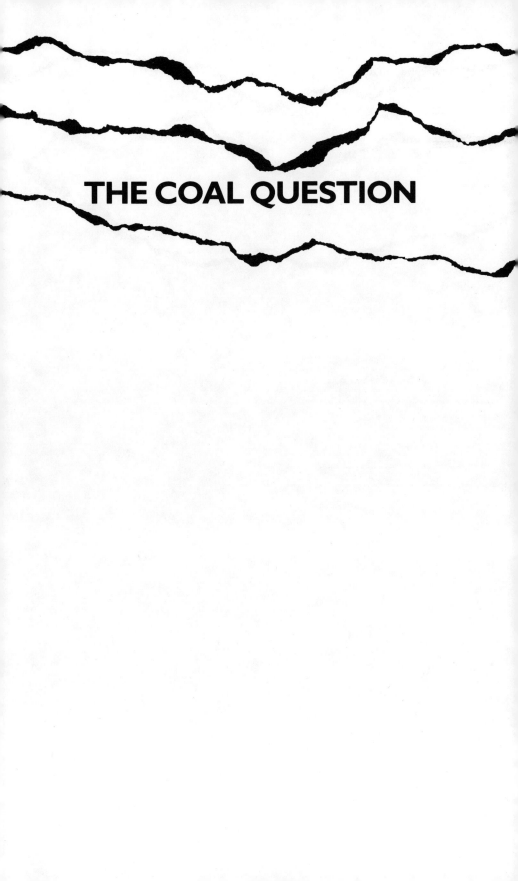

THE COAL QUESTION

THE COAL QUESTION

BY BERTHA DAVIS
AND SUSAN WHITFIELD

A GROLIER COMPANY

FRANKLIN WATTS
New York | London | Toronto | Sydney | 1982
AN IMPACT BOOK

Photographs courtesy of
Culver Pictures, Inc.: p. 14;
The Bettmann Archive: pp. 17 and 18;
United Mine Workers: p. 23;
The U.S. Department of Energy:
pp. 43 (photograph by Frank Hoffman), 53, and 62;
National Coal Association: p. 54.

Map by Vantage Art, Inc.

Library of Congress Cataloging in Publication Data

Davis, Bertha, 1910-
The coal question.

(An Impact book)
Bibliography: p.
Includes index.
Summary: Discusses the advantages and disadvantages
of using the non-renewable fossil fuel coal
as a major energy source now and in the future.
1. Coal—Juvenile literature. (1. Coal.
2. Power resources)   I. Whitfield, Susan. II. Title.
TP325.D28   662.6'2   82-4716
ISBN 0-531-04484-X   AACR2

CONTENTS

THE COAL QUESTION

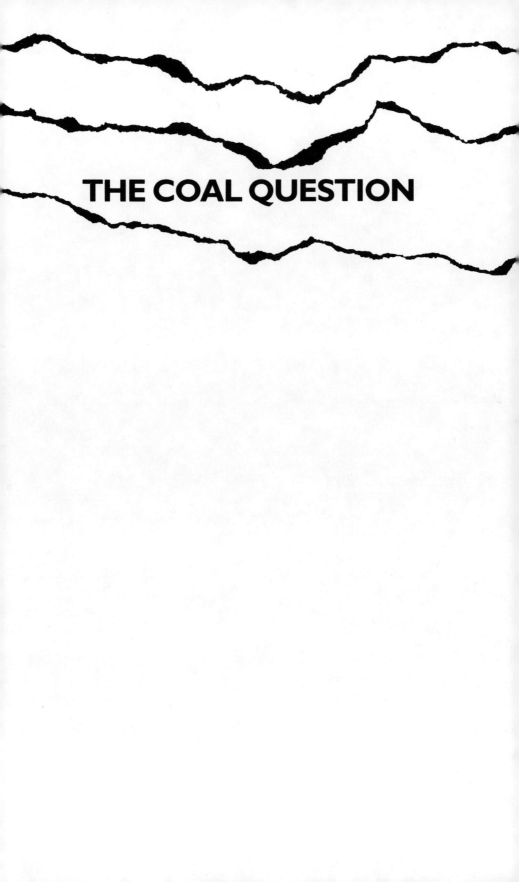

ONE

THE PROBLEM

Imagine a tank of water with a tap through which the water can be drawn. The tap is always on, sometimes drawing out more water, sometimes less, but constantly drawing something from the tank's fixed supply. What will happen to the water in the tank? The answer is obvious—it will eventually be gone.

Our planet contains a supply of fossil fuels—oil, natural gas, and coal. They were formed millions of years ago in a process so slow that we cannot hope to replace them. Thus oil, natural gas, and coal are "nonrenewable," like the water in the tank. For years, people have drawn from the earth's nonrenewable fuel supply, at first slowly and now, in our mechanized times, very rapidly.

Comparing the earth's supply of fossil fuels with the tank of water should help to make clear the seriousness of today's "energy crisis." Sometimes workers discover deposits of gas, oil, or coal that we had not known were there all along. Sometimes we draw out more fuel than we need right away, creating a "glut." Then some people think that the energy crisis is over. But the overall situation remains the same. A fixed, nonrenewable supply that is constantly drawn upon will eventually run out.

We are nearing the end of the earth's supply of fossil fuels, particularly of oil and natural gas. What lies ahead no one knows, though opinions and controversies abound. One thing is certain: Our sources of energy and our ways of using energy must soon change profoundly from what they are today.

This is a book about coal and the role it will play in the changes that lie ahead. It begins with a look at how we arrived at the present energy crisis and some possible solutions other than coal.

The "crisis" has been a long time in coming, but awareness of its coming became widespread only as recently as the 1970s. In 1973, the price of gasoline at the pump was about 35 cents per gallon. Most Americans took for granted that there was an unlimited supply of cheap fuel for their cars, furnaces, electricity, and a hundred other everyday uses. Then came the first oil shock of the 1970s.

In 1973, war broke out in the Middle East between Egypt and Israel. The United States sent military aid to its ally, Israel. To retaliate, the oil-producing Arab nations placed an embargo on oil sales to the United States and to other countries that sided with Israel. They refused, in other words, to sell oil to us and to Israel's other allies. The result was mass confusion. Long lines of impatient motorists inched their way to those gasoline stations that were selling. "Out of gas" signs went up at many more. Meat packers lost money because they could not transport their meat to markets. Shoppers often found empty shelves in food stores. Many oil-heated homes were cold that winter.

When the embargo was lifted in March 1974, the situation seemed to return to what it had been before. True, one thing had changed. The oil-producing countries had announced steep hikes in the price of their oil. But despite that higher price, it became common in the next few years to believe that our problems were over. One U.S. Congressman stated that concern over energy was "reminiscent of Chicken Little's logic."

Then, in 1978, there was a revolution in Iran, one of America's suppliers of oil. Iran's oil workers cut off oil exports. Once again, Americans experienced what it means to have a foreign power in control of the country's basic energy resource.

This state of dependence was something new. The United States had not always needed to depend on foreign countries for its main source of energy. The cutoffs of Middle Eastern oil in the 1970s created "shocks" in the United States only because a number of developments had preceded them and set the stage.

One of these developments was the decline of this country's own oil production. The first important discovery of oil in the United States came in 1859. For many years, oil deposits under U.S. soil provided enough fuel for our own needs and for extensive exports as well. But in 1970, America's oil production "peaked." That is, in 1970 we produced more oil than we ever had before; after 1970 our oil production began to decline. Like the tank of water, oil deposits under American soil had been drawn upon for over a hundred years, and the supply was running out.

Another development was the newly achieved ability of the Middle Eastern nations to control their own oil deposits. When oil was first discovered under Middle Eastern land in 1908, the countries of the Middle East did not have the technology to produce it. So U.S. oil companies, as well as oil companies from other oil-consuming nations, went into the area to look for other deposits and to take over oil production.

As years passed, the Middle Eastern nations began to resent having foreign countries in control of their oil. Iran made the first move. In 1951, it tried to take control of British Petroleum's Iranian oil holdings. The other foreign oil companies, realizing that the same thing could happen to them, acted together to defeat this take-over attempt. Since they controlled 98 percent of the world's oil refining, they were able to cripple Iran with a boycott. With no buyers for their oil, the Iranians had to agree to a settlement.

Resentment against the foreign companies grew during the 1950s. Near the end of the decade American companies felt it was necessary to lower the price of oil, which meant lower income for the Middle Eastern "host" nations. Frustrated and angry because they could do nothing about this price cut, the Middle Eastern nations decided to get together for a conference to discuss their mutual problems. Their meeting, in September 1960, produced a result of historic significance. The Organization of Petroleum Exporting Countries (OPEC) was formed. OPEC had no power at first, but its members slowly learned that by acting together they could have great power, even over the mighty oil consuming nations of the world.

Another development that contributed to the oil situation of the 1970s was the tremendous growth of this country's oil consumption. When oil was first drilled in the United States, it was used only for oil lamps. By the 1970s, our way of life required several million barrels of oil every day.

One of the reasons for the tremendous growth in U.S. oil use was that American consumers were not paying full price for the oil they were buying. In 1971, the U.S. government placed controls on all wages and prices in an attempt to control inflation. These controls included price control on oil. When the control program was ended, in 1974, oil was not included. Price control on oil remained in effect. This meant that when OPEC began announcing hikes in the price of their oil, American consumers felt little or no effect. U.S. consumers saw no reason to reduce their use of oil.

Restrictions on our oil imports also helped to set the stage for the oil shocks of the 1970s. U.S. oil production was still growing during the 1950s, but our oil was more expensive to produce than the oil of the Middle East. It could not be sold profitably at the same price as Middle Eastern oil. This created a problem. Who would buy expensive U.S. oil if they could get all they needed of cheap Middle Eastern oil? So in 1957, the U.S. government placed restrictions on the amount of foreign oil that could be imported into this country. For more than a decade, our oil production, plus these limited imports, met our energy needs.

But then, you will recall, American oil production

peaked in 1970. Soon America's declining oil production plus limited imports were no longer enough to provide for our growing oil consumption. The solution, arrived at in 1973, was to lift restrictions on imports of foreign oil. But just as the United States was preparing to buy vast additional quantities of Middle Eastern oil, the first oil shock hit, for it was also in 1973 that the Egyptian-Israeli war and the oil embargo occurred.

Thus, it was a combination of developments that led to the dependent position of the United States in 1973 and 1978. And our dependent position continues. Any time in the future, the oil-exporting nations might again decide to cut off or drastically reduce our oil supply, or announce further price hikes. That is why most Americans agree that we must do something to change this position of dependence upon foreign, often hostile, fuel suppliers.

But eliminating our dependence on imported oil is only the first stage in solving the real energy crisis. Our industries and our way of life are based on fossil fuels. And fossil fuels are being used up. Our long-range goal must be to end our dependence upon fossil fuels and to develop energy sources that can be replaced as they are used up—renewable energy sources.

A recent seven-year energy study has concluded that it will take around a hundred years to reach this long-range goal. The first fifty years will be needed to move from dependence upon imported oil to dependence upon other fuels that can serve as a bridge while we continue the transition to total use of inexhaustible sources of energy. During this long period of change, every home, machine, and powered vehicle must be replaced or converted to use a new kind of fuel. The United States will not be making this transition alone, of course. Other countries will have to make this kind of transition, too. But the United States has a special responsibility because right now we are using more than our share of the earth's nonrenewable fuels. With only 6 percent of the earth's population, we use 30 percent of the energy produced on the earth each year.

Yet we cannot move quickly into even the early stages in the transition to renewable fuels until we decide just where we are going. And on these decisions controversy erupts. Which fuels should be developed first? Which fuels can't be developed fast enough? Which fuels produce too great a risk to the environment? Which kinds of energy will cost the least? Who should pay for energy development, the government or private industry? Do we have the luxury of choosing among different kinds of energy sources or will we need to develop all kinds to meet our energy needs?

One writer states: "Although there is an energy crisis, there is no lack of energy. . . . We inhabit a planet which offers a virtually inexhaustible supply of energy." Ways of harnessing this energy were discovered long ago. But they were not fully developed because more convenient forms of energy, such as wood or later oil, were cheap and available.

Renewable sources of energy lie in, on, and around the earth. One example is the power of falling water, which can be converted into electricity (hydroelectricity). Another example is the heat that lies under the earth's crust (geo-thermal energy), which can be brought to the surface in pipes and used directly for heating or converted into electricity. Just one mile underground, the temperature is about 100°F hotter than it is at the surface, and it becomes increasingly hot farther down toward the earth's core. The oceans offer a vast resource of renewable energy. One example is "ocean thermal" energy, in which very cold water is brought up from the ocean floor and used in contrast with the sun-warmed surface water to drive a turbine and produce electricity.

Some renewable energy sources are in limited use right now. But none has been developed as fully as it could be. Hydropower, for example, lost importance as fossil fuels and, later, nuclear power gained importance. But if all the sources of hydropower in just the state of New York were harnessed, they could produce as much electricity as three or four nuclear power stations.

Most of the renewable energy sources are considered part of the broad field of solar energy. One example of the use of solar energy, solar heating, is gaining rapidly in importance. Solar heating takes two major forms. A building designed with large windows facing south to trap the winter sun's heat is using what is called "passive" solar heating. This way of using the sun's energy is nothing new. The American Indians of Mesa Verde, Colorado, applied this principle eight hundred years ago in designing their cliff dwellings. Over the centuries, other societies applied the passive solar heating principle too. But, like hydropower, passive solar design declined in popularity when oil became cheaply available.

"Active" solar heating, on the other hand, uses modern technology. It generally involves roof panels, placed at an angle to collect the maximum amount of winter sunshine. The solar heat is then concentrated and stored until it is needed. Although many people doubted that solar heat could really keep their homes warm even when the sun was not shining, this attitude is changing. As one industry leader put it recently, "People don't think about whether solar works anymore; they think about when they can afford it."

This remark points up an important barrier to solar energy playing a major role in the period of transition to renewable fuels—expense. True, the fuel for solar energy, unlike the fuel for most other forms of energy, is free. But equipment must be purchased to convert that free sunshine into useful energy. And further research is needed before this equipment can be produced for a price that the average homeowner can afford to pay.

Another form of solar energy would remove from individual homeowners the burden of buying equipment. It is called solar thermal electric power. This is solar power on a big scale. Here, acres of mirrors are placed at angles so that they reflect a great deal of sunlight and beam its concentrated heat onto one central boiler. Steam from that boiler drives a turbine and produces electricity. The electricity

can then be sold to homeowners just like electricity produced by more conventional means. But, unlike the technology for small-scale solar heating, the technology for
solar thermal electricity requires much more research to
make it work efficiently. It offers a possible long-range energy solution but probably could not become part of the
energy bridge for at least another fifteen to twenty years.

Solar energy's most promising contribution to the energy bridge, and to the final energy solution, may turn out to
be photovoltaic cells. These cells, made mostly of silicon,
convert sunlight directly into electricity. They might be used
by individual homeowners or by large utility companies that
sell the electricity to consumers. Photovoltaic technology is
already advanced; the remaining problem is that it is still
too expensive to compete with other energy sources.

The Reagan administration proposes to lower the
amount of government money going into solar energy
development, a change of course that has produced
sharply different reactions. Some solar industrialists fear that
without greater funding, America's solar industry will fall
behind that of other countries, especially Japan. One bank-
er noted: "If the Japanese really get a strong patent position worldwide, where are we going to get our photovol-
taics from? In ten years this is going to be a billion dollar a
year business."

But others feel that less government support will actually benefit the solar industry. This is true, they say, because
the solar industry has attracted some participants who are
more enthusiastic than knowledgeable. They have produced poor products that made people believe that solar
energy did not really work. Without government grants,
they say, only the solar companies producing truly efficient
products will stay in business. And this will convince more
people that solar energy is effective. As one solar industrialist put it: "Business executives, telecommunications companies, utilities, hydroelectric companies are going to start
to see us more as a business now, not as a hobby, not as a
ban-the-nukes/save-the-whales bunch of guys who stand
around airports and pass out literature."

It is true that many people still believe that solar energy does not offer a serious solution to the energy problem. This is one point in the heated controversy between supporters of solar energy and supporters of nuclear energy.

Nuclear energy provokes probably the greatest controversy over whether it could, or even should, serve as a bridge fuel or as part of the final solution to the energy crisis. A government official states that: "As you look across the horizon to find answers to our energy problems there's no real place to turn in the next 30 years other than nuclear to keep us from being all hostages to foreign countries." But a recent Harvard Business School energy study takes exactly the opposite position, stating that "In the United States there is simply no reasonable possibility for massive contributions from nuclear power for at least the rest of the twentieth century."

Safety is the main issue standing in the way of nuclear energy. The possible catastrophe of "meltdown" (a nuclear reactor core breaking down and burning its way through the earth) was the subject of a popular motion picture of the 1970s called *The China Syndrome*. The film happened to be playing in theaters just when an actual accident took place in the nuclear power plant at Three Mile Island, Pennsylvania. Concern over the risks of nuclear energy became widespread and emotional.

The government is forcing the nuclear industry to meet safety requirements to lower the risk of such accidents. Meeting these increasingly strict safety standards has slowed the growth of nuclear energy. Adding safety features makes the power plants much more expensive to build than had been expected. Plants that fail to meet the safety regulations are not allowed to operate. This added expense and the need to pass a growing list of safety requirements has forced some plants to close down and has discouraged industrialists from beginning construction on new ones.

Yet nuclear energy's most serious safety problem may be disposing of its radioactive waste products. Nuclear power plants were originally planned to reprocess these wastes. But this produces an otherwise very scarce material, plutonium, that can be used in making atom bombs. Keeping track of every bit of plutonium would be difficult, and nuclear critics fear that some could be stolen by terrorists to produce an atom bomb with which to threaten a country or the world.

The plutonium risk caused the government to ban reprocessing radioactive wastes. They have instead been temporarily stored near the power plants. So far, no one has been able to come up with a completely acceptable plan for permanently disposing of the dangerous radioactive wastes.

The Reagan administration proposes to remove the barriers that have blocked the progress of nuclear development. It plans to drop regulations that many people feel are excessive. It proposes reversing the ban on reprocessing nuclear wastes as a solution to the growing waste disposal problem. And it will raise the amount of government money going into development of nuclear energy.

This plan is based upon the belief that nuclear energy's safety risks have been greatly exaggerated. It is also based upon the view that development of nuclear energy is necessary to free us from dependence upon foreign oil. But critics claim that it is not necessary for us to have nuclear power, because it can only be used to produce electricity, and electricity can be produced in many ways that do not involve the risks of nuclear power. One physicist who holds this view made this comparison: "Using nuclear power to produce electricity is the equivalent of using a chain saw to cut butter."

Solar and nuclear energy are not the only possible alternatives, especially for the near future. After the oil shocks of the 1970s the U.S. government removed controls from the price of oil to encourage the increased production of our own oil supplies. If American oil companies were receiving higher prices, it would be profitable for them to search for hard-to-reach deposits of fuel that still lie under our own land.

The result has been a boom in oil exploration in the United States. Workers are returning to drilling sites they had not considered worth bothering with during the days of cheap Middle Eastern oil. One area used to be called a "driller's graveyard" because so many holes had to be drilled there before any oil could be found. This is a very expensive process. But now, the prospect of huge profits has brought workers back to the driller's graveyard to try again. Increased production of U.S. oil may help free us from dependence upon foreign oil for a limited time. But, of course, it offers no long-range solution.

Decontrolling oil prices has had another result. It has encouraged the development of an energy resource that few people even think of as an energy resource. This resource has made it possible for the United States to lower oil imports from 8.5 million barrels per day in August 1979 to 5.2 million barrels per day in August 1981. This energy resource is conservation. Higher prices have forced Americans to begin learning to consume less oil. One comparison reveals just how powerful an energy resource conservation has proved to be. In 1979 the U.S. government proposed to spend billions on a program to produce oil substitutes. It was hoped that these substitutes would lower oil imports by 2.5 million barrels per day by 1990. In contrast to this, conservation lowered oil imports by more than that—by 3.3 million barrels per day—in just two years. And conservation costs nothing! Conservation must be part of the bridge period and perhaps the final energy picture. But at best it can be only a partial solution.

Then there is coal. Like oil and natural gas, our fixed supply of coal will eventually be used up. But, unlike those of oil and natural gas, our remaining supplies of coal are vast. Experts tell us that, at our present rate of consumption, our coal could last at least another two hundred years. If coal use is increased as much as possible, our supply would still last around a hundred years. Coal looks like the obvious solution, at least during the long transition to inexhaustible fuels.

Yet our present use of coal is far less than it could be. And there is great controversy over how big a role coal should play in the future. To understand coal's special status, and to arrive at a thoughtful judgment on what its future should be in the transition to renewable fuels, it is helpful to go back and trace coal's energy history.

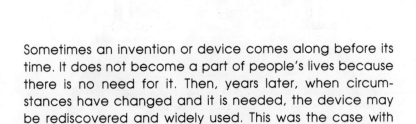

TWO

THE HISTORY OF COAL

Sometimes an invention or device comes along before its time. It does not become a part of people's lives because there is no need for it. Then, years later, when circumstances have changed and it is needed, the device may be rediscovered and widely used. This was the case with the steam engine.

A simple form of the steam engine was first invented almost two thousand years ago by an ancient Greek named Hero. But Hero's steam engine was used only to create magical effects in the temples to awe the worshippers. No one thought of developing it as a machine to do work because, in those days, there were plenty of slaves for that.

Hero's description of his invention was translated into English in 1575. By that time, people were interested in using powered machines to perform work. So inventors began trying to apply Hero's ideas. By 1698, they had developed a steam-powered pump nicknamed "The Miner's Friend" because it could pump water out of mine shafts. A better name might have been "The Mine *Owner's* Friend" because, with the shafts cleared of water, the miners could go far deeper into the mine pits and haul out even greater amounts of coal.

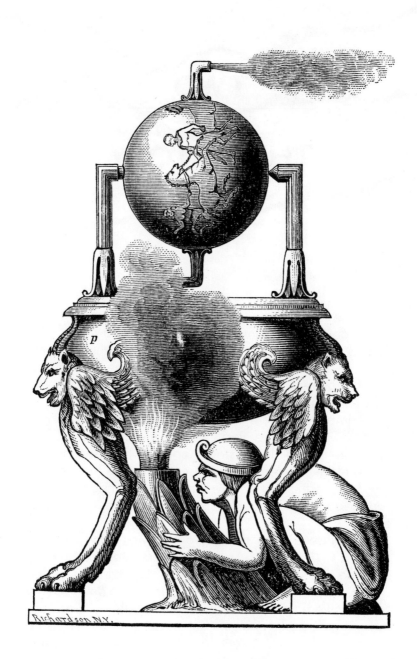

Hero's steam engine.

In the 1600s, coal was already in use for heating in those parts of Europe where the supply of trees was running out. Further inventions then led to a great new importance for coal. In 1709, Abraham Darby invented a way to make iron using coal instead of charcoal. This made possible a boom in iron production, because charcoal, made from wood, was in limited supply, but there was plenty of coal. Finally, in 1769, James Watt developed a more efficient version of the steam engine, using coal to produce the steam that powered the engine.

More and more jobs were performed by these steam engines. Factories were built to house the engines. People moved away from rural areas to get jobs in the factories and in the coal mines that supplied the factories' fuel. This great change in the way people lived and worked is called the Industrial Revolution.

Exactly what role coal played in the Industrial Revolution is a source of controversy. Many writers say that coal made it possible. But one scholar states: "The notion that a handful of British inventors suddenly made the wheels hum in the eighteenth century is too crude even to dish up as a fairy tale to children. . . . Plainly, the industrial revolution would have come into existence and gone on steadily had not a ton of coal been dug."

This is because steam was not the only way of powering machines in the eighteenth century. For years, wind and water had been used. Wind and water drove machines that did some of the work of making iron. They also ground grain, sawed wood, pumped water, spun thread, wove cloth, and more. Areas with strong winds and rapid rivers became manufacturing centers.

And in that fact lay the drawback to wind and water as sources of power, for until further inventions came along, they could be used only in places where the wind or the water currents were strong enough to drive machines. It was not until the nineteenth century that the water turbine and electricity made it possible for water power to be used in factories far away.

In the meantime, the invention of the steam engine had made industrialists turn away from wind and water power. The steam engine could be used wherever its fuel (usually coal) could be transported. So coal and the steam engine became the driving forces of a great new industrial growth.

Coal use became widespread in the United States more than a hundred years later than it did in Europe. This is because the long-established European countries had used up a great deal of their supply of wood, while forests were still plentiful in the United States, a new country.

The early story of coal in the United States has been called a "battle to win acceptance for coal in America." America's first coal mining company was formed in Pennsylvania right after the Revolutionary War. In the 1790s, some adventurous Philadelphia businessmen, convinced that America was ready to join Europe's coal boom, formed the Lehigh Coal Mine Company. But nobody would buy or use their coal, and the company failed. Years later, when America was indeed ready for coal, the successors to the Lehigh Coal Company made fortunes.

It was not until 1808 that coal was first tried as a heating fuel in America. A special grate was constructed for Judge Jesse Fell of Wilkes-Barre, Pennsylvania. He wrote: "I made the experiment of burning the common stone coal of the valley in a grate, in a fireplace in my house, and found it will answer the purpose of a fuel, making a cleaner and better fire at less expense than burning wood in the common way."

This is an advertisement for a portable steam engine introduced in 1849. By this time, many models of steam engine were on the market.

A. L. ARCHAMBAULT'S
PORTABLE STEAM ENGINE,
(ON WHEELS, OR WITHOUT,)
FIRST INTRODUCED, JULY, 1849.

Four Silver Medals & Six Diplomas, by Franklin Inst. & other Exhibitions.

These Engines can be built from 4 to 30 horse-power, and are used for various purposes, such as

WORKING OIL WELLS,
Driving Threshing Machines,
Circular Saw Mills, Ore Washers.

Also arranged with Drum

FOR HOISTING, PILE DRIVING, ETC.

The above cut will give you a good representation of the 10, 12 and 15 horse-powers. They were first introduced in the oil regions in 1861. A large number have been sent to OIL CITY, FRANKLIN and WESTERN VIRGINIA. and have given entire satisfaction.

☞ *Please call at the Works,* **Cor. Beach & Vienna Sts.,** *and see them ready to ship.*

**Sheffield, England, chokes in the fumes
of the Industrial Revolution.**

This was taken as a sensational discovery, and Judge Fell's neighbors had similar grates built. Some enterprising businessman loaded coal onto a barge and floated it down the Susquehana River to Columbia, Pennsylvania. But here, no one knew about Judge Fell's "discovery," and at first nobody would buy the coal. The "black stones" had to be left behind in a dump heap. The following year, the businessman returned with more coal plus one of Judge Fell's grates. Convinced that the black stones would really burn, the people bought the coal.

Even development of the steam engine did not immediately lead to increased coal production in America, as it had in Europe. With plenty of wood still available, charcoal was used to power the steam engine and to make iron. Some manufacturers tried using coal but rejected it because they said it "put the fire out." One angry industrialist buried the coal he had ordered, and others ground it up to use for gravel.

But intensive sales efforts, plus the rising price for wood, helped coal gain acceptance. By 1875, coal and wood each provided about 45 percent of the fuel supply of the United States. By 1900, that percentage had risen to 89 percent.

An Industrial Revolution might have come without coal, but coal was directly responsible for many of the ways in which life changed during the Industrial Revolution. The industrial town became almost an extension of the coal mine. Since transporting coal was costly, heavy industries were usually built near coal seams. Here, too, were the houses companies built for their workers. There was no escape from the sights and smells of mines and factories.

To these bleak valleys came people who had recently emigrated to the United States and others who could find no other means of making a living. Work in the mines was hard and dangerous. A frequent sight in the mine town was the wagon that served as an ambulance or a hearse, carrying a miner on his last trip from the mine shaft to his front door, or the miners' wives huddled around the mine entrance late at night, waiting for the bodies of their husbands to be brought to the surface.

Great bitterness and suspicion existed between the miners and the mine owners. In 1868, a union was formed to give the workers greater strength in dealing with their employers. In 1875, the union went on strike to protest dramatic cuts in miners' wages. As the long strike progressed, the miners, with no wages at all, became desperately poor. One miner wrote: "Since I saw you last I have buried our youngest child, and on the day before its death there was not a bit of food in the house with six children." Eventually, the miners had to give up and return to work on the owners' terms.

After the unsuccessful strike of 1875, many mysterious acts of violence broke out in the coalfields. These crimes were supposedly committed by a secret society of miners called the Molly Maguires. The coal mine owners hired a detective named James McParlan, who posed as a fugitive from justice and won the confidence of this society. After several months, McParlan testified in court against the Molly Maguires, and ten of them were hanged. Peace and order were restored to the coalfields.

This is a very controversial chapter in coal's history. Many historians believe that McParlan was hired to get rid of innocent miners who were influential among the others and encouraged the protests. The Sherlock Holmes mystery, "The Valley of Fear," was based on actual events in the Molly Maguire incident, though it gives a very different interpretation of those events.

As the nation's dependence upon coal grew, so did the strength of the coal miners' union. By 1920, coal fueled America's railroads, ships, iron and steel furnaces, and home-heating furnaces. It supplied most of America's electrical energy. A national strike by the 400,000 unionized coal miners could cripple the nation, and the miners knew it.

A former miner, John L. Lewis, won control of the United

Mine Workers union (UMW) and led it through battles with mine owners that brought many benefits to the miners and for a time made the UMW the most feared union in America. Lewis controlled the union for forty years and was a very controversial figure.

Perhaps the controversies between the union and the mine owners raged most strongly during World War II. There was a great demand for coal to supply America's military needs, and the miners producing that coal wanted higher wages. Lewis claimed that the government "fattens industry and starves labor, and then calls upon labor patriotically to starve." Several times the miners struck for higher wages. The president of the United States warned: "The continuance and spread of these strikes would have the same effect on the course of the war as a crippling defeat in the battlefield." The federal government actually took over the mines for a while during 1946, but the strikes continued and were finally settled with some concessions for the miners. Lewis became one of the most hated public figures in the country. But to the miners, he was a hero.

As the demand for coal declined, so did the power of the UMW. But labor unrest continues to have an enormous effect upon the fortunes of the coal industry.

Other elements of the coal boom years remain as part of American life. One is the railroad. In several ways the railroad was a product of the mine. As far back as the 1500s, in Germany, heavy carts were placed on wooden rails so they could be moved over the rough surface of the mine floors. In the 1700s, iron rails replaced the wooden ones. Later, coal-driven steam engines pulled the cars over the rails. The coal-powered railroad, in turn, pulled huge loads of coal from the mines to consumers. Railroad transportation made widespread use of coal possible. Only years later was the railroad used to transport passengers. Similarly the elevator was first used to haul miners up the mine shafts.

Even as coal was becoming the major source of power for America's industrial growth, other events were setting the stage for coal's downfall. In the middle of the nine-teenth century, most American homes were illuminated by whale oil lamps. In fact, so many whales had been killed for their oil that they were becoming scarce, and whale oil was becoming expensive. A substitute was needed.

Some Connecticut businessmen sent Edwin Drake to drill for petroleum to serve this purpose. Drake struck oil in 1859. Commenting on this event, one modern scholar states: "Smart people thought we were entering a period when petroleum was to light the lamps of the world. There was no other known use for petroleum at that time. But, of course, these people were wrong." The development of electricity soon provided the substitute for whale oil illumi-nation. And another invention led to a vast, unexpected role for Drake's petroleum. This was the internal combustion engine.

A long competition began between the coal-powered steam engine and the oil-powered internal combustion engine. Plants producing electricity, industrial machines, and railroads could use either coal or oil for fuel. But oil offered the great advantage of relative lightness and transportability. New inventions such as the automobile and the airplane opened up vast markets for oil where coal could not compete. The airplane never would have gotten off the ground if it had had to lug along enough coal to keep its engines running.

Electricity, as well as petroleum, freed industry from its dependence upon coal. Factories no longer had to be located near coal seams or railroad lines that hauled the coal. Electricity could carry power from its source to even faraway plants. And electricity could be produced by a variety of fuels, not just coal.

Electricity provided even greater flexibility within the factories. For once a coal fire was lit, the machines it pow-ered had to keep working constantly to avoid wasting fuel. But electric-powered motors could be turned on or off as they were needed. Coal was no longer the most efficient industrial power source.

John L. Lewis (1880–1969),
for many years the head of the UMW.

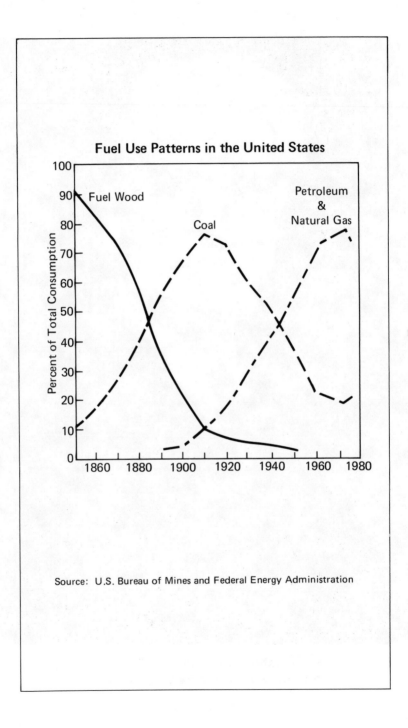

Fuel Use Patterns in the United States

Source: U.S. Bureau of Mines and Federal Energy Administration

As if competition from oil were not enough, coal soon began to have serious competition from another fuel, natural gas. In the beginning of the nineteenth century, long before the development of electricity for illumination, coal was used to produce synthetic gas for lighting. By the end of the nineteenth century, coal gas was also widely used for cooking. But this manufactured gas was expensive and could no longer compete when natural gas was discovered in the southwestern United States. Natural gas became increasingly popular as people developed additional ways of using it and improved pipelines transported it to even faraway consumers.

In the 1960s, it looked as if the strongest competitor of all was going to be a new source of energy, nuclear energy. In 1966, a nuclear scientist announced: "Nuclear reactors now appear to be the cheapest of all sources of energy." Early nuclear developers expected that by the 1980s there would be hundreds of nuclear power plants producing a quarter of America's electricity. But these optimistic predictions turned out to be wrong. Instead, a spirited competition developed between coal and nuclear power to produce electricity for the nation's utility companies.

The competition just described is part of the explanation for the downward slope of the graph opposite. Two other causes contributed to the twentieth century drop in coal use. One was its price. Coal was a more expensive fuel than its rivals, oil and natural gas. The second was its characteristics as a fuel. This will be fully discussed in Chapter Three, so we will simply note now that the pollution caused by burning coal won it many enemies.

The coal story in the United States is summed up in the graph opposite. Although milestones such as the development of the steam engine or the automobile surely had great influence, the graph shows how slowly change really occurred. Experts say that it takes at least fifty years to convert from one fuel source to another. It is not just that machines must be converted to use a new fuel, but people's tastes must change, too, as the story of the battle to win acceptance for coal has shown. Surprising developments may have great influence, as did the unexpected use for Drake's petroleum in combustion engines. And something that has been around a long time may turn out to be just what is needed when circumstances have changed.

The story of coal in the United States, in fact, contains many lessons about energy development and use that may help us work out a solution to our present energy crisis.

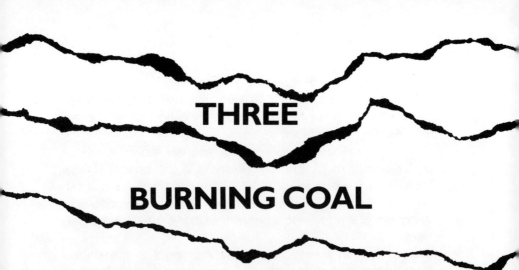

THREE

BURNING COAL

As you just read in the preceding chapter, coal had to make a place for itself in the fuel market of the nineteenth century. Now, again, the coal industry strives to grow. How successful can it be? How successful should it be? How successful will it be? These three questions form the framework for this chapter and the next.

No one questions the abundance of coal in the United States. This abundance is most impressive when U.S. coal reserves are compared with its reserves of other fuels. To make comparisons among different kinds of reserves, one or two technical terms relating to energy must be introduced. One cannot compare barrels with tons. It is essential to translate the quantities these terms represent into a common unit of measure. The common unit that is used in the energy field measures a fuel's heat-producing capacity. The heat-producing capacity of any fuel is expressed in British thermal units (Btu's). A Btu is the amount of heat it takes to raise the temperature of one pound of water 1° Fahrenheit. Different types of coal will yield different amounts of Btu's per ton, but on the average coal yields about 22,800,000; petroleum produces about 5,800,000 Btu's per barrel. It is simply a matter of arithmetic, therefore, to convert the "known recoverable reserves" of each of the fuel resources of the United States into the Btu's locked within those reserves. ("Known recoverable reserves" means the reserves that are known and can be extracted with existing technology.)

Here is the comparison. Coal reserves make up about 81.7 percent of all the fuel reserves in the United States. Shale oil is a weak second with 7 percent, natural gas follows with 3.5 percent, petroleum with 2.8 percent, and other potential energy resources make up the remaining 5 percent.

But the undisputed availability of coal in the United States does not automatically guarantee the coal industry's growth. Only growth in *demand* for coal generates growth in the industry, and in the years since the oil shocks of the 1970s, that surge of demand has failed to come.

As a matter of fact, the U.S. coal industry has been in trouble since the late seventies. Operating mines can produce much more than the market, at this time, is absorbing. Many small mines have gone bankrupt in the last few years. True, things began to look up in the early 1980s. U.S. production and use of coal increased, and coal exports increased. But the industry continued to face serious problems.

Why are we not using more coal? Why is it not taken for granted that coal is at least the short-term answer to the energy problem in the United States? The basic reason was summed up by one observer in words to this effect: Coal is dirty—dirty to mine, dirty to transport, and dirty to burn. The last point is by far the most important. It is principally in relation to the burning of coal that serious questions arise about whether or not we should, even though we can, increase its use. One of the chief obstacles to coal's increased use in the energy market, in other words, is the effect of coal use upon air quality.

When coal is burned, certain solids and gases are emitted, or released, from the burners—sulfur oxides (primarily in the form of sulfur dioxide), nitrogen oxides, carbon oxides, and particulates. "Particulates" is the term used for the solid material that enters the air from coal combustion (burning).

Concern about sulfur oxides in the air is based on our knowledge that they can cause serious illnesses such as emphysema and chronic bronchitis. Crops and other plants, too, can be affected by sulfur oxides. Some materials corrode when exposed to air polluted in this way. We know less about the effects of nitrogen oxides in the air, but their connection with certain respiratory ailments is being increasingly noted.

Two other effects of burning coal are important among the arguments against wider use of coal. The first effect is "acid rain." Oxides of sulfur and nitrogen form a weak acid solution when they combine with moisture in the atmosphere. When this moisture falls as rain, there is a measurable degree of acidity in it. This acidity is harmful to plant and animal life.

The effects of acid rain have been dramatic in the northeastern United States and Canada. More than two hundred lakes in these areas already contain over ten times the normal levels of acidity. Here the fish have all but died out. Every year, the level of acidity, and the number of dead or dying lakes, grows. Scientists have traced the cause to factory emissions from industries in the Midwest that are carried eastward by the prevailing westerly winds and that fall in rain over these northeastern lakes and forests.

The coal industry protests that it is being given too much of the blame for acid rain. An equally important cause, they claim, is emissions from automobile exhausts. Outside the coal industry there are those who claim that the danger of acid rain has been exaggerated. One government official even called the concern over acid rain "another scare tactic" of the environmentalists.

The second effect brought up against coal burning is the buildup of carbon dioxide (CO_2) in the atmosphere. All fossil fuels contain carbon. They all give off CO_2 when they burn, but coal gives off 25 percent more CO_2 than oil and

67 percent more than gas. There is, however, another cause that can be associated with the CO_2 buildup. In recent years, thousands of square miles of forests, which remove CO_2 from the air, have been cut down. But it is impossible to determine which of the two—fossil fuel combustion or deforestation—is the more important reason for the buildup.

Measurement of the amount of carbon dioxide in the atmosphere has been going on since 1958. It shows an increase of 7 percent since that year in the amount of CO_2. A recent World Climate Conference reported general agreement on two other figures: that the CO_2 in the atmosphere has increased 18 percent in the last century and that it is currently increasing at the rate of about 0.4 percent per year.

Some meteorologists predict that within the next hundred years this CO_2 buildup will cause great changes in the earth's climate. CO_2 in the atmosphere surrounding the earth will block the escape of heat into space. Called the "greenhouse effect," this buildup of heat due to increased levels of CO_2 could result in warming of the earth's surface, the scientists say, perhaps causing the polar ice caps to melt and raising the levels of the oceans, which would then flood coastal cities.

Many people believe this tremendous risk to all countries on the earth forces us to limit the amount of coal we burn. But one scientist, suggesting that we should not let fear of CO_2 buildup affect our energy plans, dismissed the problem this way: "We do not know enough to say what amount of increase of carbon dioxide is safe, and would be unsuccessful if we tried to enforce any such global limit. By the time we were certain that a carbon dioxide-caused climate change was occurring, it would be too late to prevent it."

In the peak years of its use, coal was known to have some of the undesirable qualities that have just been described. But homes and industries went right on using enormous quantities of it. People only began to abandon coal when cleaner-burning oil became available at a price lower than coal's.

Since the oil shocks of the seventies the price situation has turned right around again, this time in coal's favor. The delivered price of coal at the present time varies from place to place, from one-fifth the price of a comparable amount of oil to one-half the price. But the market has responded only slightly to coal's price advantage. For some new things have been added. Now there is the federal Clean Air Act. And there are state and local clean air laws. And finally, there is the federal Environmental Protection Agency (EPA), charged with carrying out this new clean air legislation.

To do this, the EPA has established standards that limit the emission into the air of seven major classes of pollutants: particulates, sulfur dioxide, carbon monoxide, ozone, hydrocarbons, nitrogen dioxide, and lead. The amounts of these pollutants that fuel-using units and fuel-using activities may release into the air is specifically limited. Naming a specific quantity of each pollutant that emissions may not exceed is sometimes referred to as the "threshold" approach. Go beyond this threshold, so the argument goes, and you enter the stage where the pollutant becomes harmful.

The limits vary in different situations and in different areas. For example, the standards that govern existing coal-burning units are less strict than those for new units. An existing coal-burning unit in an area whose air quality is good has to meet higher standards than an existing unit in a lower air quality area.

This is because a central goal of the federal clean air legislation is to "prevent significant deterioration (worsening)" of any area's air quality. Areas that already were highly industrialized when the Clean Air Act was passed in 1970 could not immediately clean up their air to equal that of a residential community or a wilderness park. They needed standards that gave them time.

There is general agreement that different standards for

different places is a sensible idea, but controversy often erupts when the principle is put into practice.

The EPA has established 247 different Air Quality Control Regions. State and local governments share with the federal government responsibility for enforcing, in these regions, local, state, and federal clean air laws.

The federal threshold levels mentioned above are set forth as primary standards (considered necessary to protect public health) and secondary standards (considered necessary to protect the natural environment). Threshold levels are also expressed as short-term standards (governing emissions during 24-hour periods) and long-term standards (governing total emissions over a year). Areas that meet the standards set for them are called "attainment areas," while those that do not yet come up to standard are classified as "nonattainment areas." In short, present and potential users of coal must accept the fact that coal must "burn clean" or it cannot be burned.

Coal can "burn clean." Or at least it can burn clean enough to meet the EPA's standards. Sulfur dioxide emission standards, for example, are the ones of greatest concern to coal users, and there are many ways to meet those standards. Existing coal-burning plants in some areas can, simply by changing to the use of low-sulfur coal, reduce their sulfur emissions sufficiently to meet federal and local standards. The industry calls this using "compliance coal,"

More frequently, however, pollution-control equipment is needed to meet air quality standards. The most commonly used equipment is the flue-gas desulferizer, the so-called scrubber. Scrubbers are devices that chemically remove sulfur dioxide from the fumes released when coal is burned. There are many different scrubbing systems, but they all remove the sulfur gases from the smokestacks of plants. In other words, they remove the sulfur compounds after they are formed during combustion.

Scrubbers are effective but expensive to install. In addition, the desulferization process by which a scrubber cleans up the emissions from burning coal creates a soupy white sludge. This sludge contains chemicals that can work their way into the ground, with possible harmful effects upon ground water. So the sludge must be disposed of in acceptable ways, and that means additional cost.

Other ways of handling the sulfur dioxide problem are available. One approach is to reduce the amount of sulfur in the coal *before* it is burned. There is a "washing," or cleaning, process that can remove the sulfur that is combined with the iron particles in the coal, but this process does not remove the organic sulfur that is chemically bound to the hydrocarbons that make up coal. The technology to get out this organic sulfur is not yet available but is being worked on.

Another approach is to catch the sulfur while the burning is taking place. In "fluidized-bed combustion," crushed coal is burned over a bed of limestone in a stream of air. During the burning, the sulfur combines with the calcium in the limestone to form a solid that drops down in the burner unit and is removed with the ashes. Some results are in from plants that are trying out this method of burning coal. These results suggest that the process may be sufficiently developed for profitable use in small industrial boilers in the not too distant future. But fluidized-bed combustion is a long way from being the answer for large utility plants.

Any and all of these approaches to controlling pollution from coal combustion are costly. The 1977 amendments to the Clean Air Act require that all new large coal-fired boilers must install the "best available control technology" regardless of the sulfur content of the coal they burn. Under the best available technology requirements, boilers must have scrubbers and "baghouses," which are fabric filters used to remove particulates. Critics of this last requirement point out that, while the filters do remove 99 percent of the particulates from the boiler's emissions, they do not hold back the smallest, dustlike particles. The cost of installing and maintaining these controls varies from 15 percent of all the money a company spends on erecting and operating a plant to over one-third of its expenses.

So, looking again at the question of why we are not using more coal, part of the answer should now be clear. Concern for clean air has made coal use a tightly controlled and very expensive enterprise. It must be noted at this point that not everyone agrees with the policies that are now being followed to achieve cleaner air. A recent study sponsored by a major foundation specifically attacks the threshold approach to defining levels of pollution and recommends that it be abandoned. This controversy will be treated in Chapter Seven, so, for the present, we will just say this: A battle may be raging over the way we are going about the business of getting cleaner air, but there is no battle over the *goal* of cleaner air, and the day of unregulated coal use is undoubtedly over.

Can coal, in this regulated setting, expand its share of the fuel market? This big question opens up a series of other questions that will have to be tackled one at a time. Who are the best customers for the coal industry at the present time? Could they become better customers? What industries that are not now coal customers could become coal customers? Can the industry sell more coal to other countries of the industrial world that share our desire to shift away from dependence upon imported oil? Will a syn-fuels industry open up an important new market for coal?

These questions are the subject of the next chapter.

FOUR

SELLING COAL

At present, coal supplies about 20 percent of this country's energy needs. Of the coal used, about 80 percent is burned by utility companies to produce electricity. The other 20 percent is used by other industries. The coal that goes to the utility companies supplied, in 1978, about 44 percent of their energy needs.

The public utility industry, in other words, is by far the coal industry's biggest customer, even though that industry at present uses coal for less than half its energy needs. The coal industry would like to increase that percentage. If any significant portion of the utilities that now use oil-fired boilers converted to coal, coal production would soar. If the public utility industry were to grow, and if the new plants built to meet that expanding market for electricity chose coal instead of alternative fuels, coal production would have to expand enormously.

Utilities are using more coal than they had been. But the displacement of oil by coal in the utility industry is not happening as widely and rapidly as had been hoped by coal industrialists.

Ten years ago one would not have written, "If the public utility industry were to grow." That industry's growth rate over the years had been remarkably consistent—between 7 and 7.5 percent per year, year after year. Since 1973, that reliable pattern of growth has drastically changed, a change that most experts say had two causes. They point to the slowdown in industrial growth generally, and they stress the impact of conservation practices upon use of electric power. There will be more about this second point later.

If and when growth in the public utility industry does come, coal seems to be in the best position to take advantage of it. For one thing, the U.S. government has taken steps to encourage coal use. The Powerplant and Industrial Fuel Use Act of 1978 prohibited the use of oil and natural gas in new large boilers. The Energy Tax Act of 1978 allows coal-using industries to make some deductions from their income that are not allowed if other fuels are used. This means lower income taxes for coal users.

Coal will also undoubtedly benefit from the difficulties that nuclear energy is encountering. The movement of nuclear power into the utility field, into any field for that matter, seems to be almost at a standstill because of public concern over safety problems and growing costs. Since the Three Mile Island accident in March 1979, the nuclear industry has received not one order for a reactor from a public utility company.

Conversion of existing boilers to coal need not wait for an expanding market. Why hasn't the shift from oil to coal burners been happening at the rate expected? Government policy has certainly encouraged it, but few conversions have actually been made. In some studies of the industry, it is claimed that while legislation calls for conversion to coal, the same legislation lists many exceptions, under which dozens of companies are relieved of the obligation and expense of converting.

Also, the government procedures connected with conversion are complex and time-consuming. It sometimes appears that agencies within the government are working in less than complete harmony. The conversion legislation, called the Energy Supply Act, was passed in 1974, and in the next three years the Federal Energy Administration, forerunner of the Department of Energy, ordered seventy-four electric utility plants to convert to coal. These seventy-four companies went to great expense to carry out the orders, but only fifteen of them got through the machinery of approval of the EPA during those three years so they could begin operating again.

Several utility companies have gone through several conversions—from coal to oil and then back to coal again. An official in one of these companies warned that it is simply not realistic to expect rapid, widespread conversion because so much is involved. "It's well worth it in the end," he said, "but sometimes there doesn't seem to be any end in sight."

In addition to the too-much-red-tape, too-many-regulations arguments, utilities make another point in defending their reluctance to convert. They would find it difficult, they claim, to raise the money needed to cover the costs of conversion. Utility companies must go to their state utility commissions for permission to raise rates to cover the expenses of conversion. If the commission refuses to give a company that permission, conversion, so far as that company is concerned, is a dead issue.

Supporters of conversion attack the public utility commissions that refuse to permit this pass-through of costs. They claim that consumers would benefit in the long run from the conversion. The temporary increase in rates to cover the costs of conversion, they say, should not be allowed to stand in the way of the long-term benefit consumers would receive when the utilities were able to burn cheap coal instead of expensive oil.

The final argument that utilities have used against conversion to coal is that they must have a reliable fuel supply. The coal industry, they claim, because of its history of labor strife, has not always been a reliable supplier. This point will be discussed in Chapter Five.

One might think that cheap coal versus expensive oil would drive the utilities to convert. But critics of the industry say that the utilities have not felt that pressure. The high fuel costs they complain of are not really hurting to the point of driving them to do something. The public service commissions have been fairly consistent in allowing the utilities to pass along the higher fuel costs to their customers.

What are coal's chances of finding a bigger market in industries other than the public utility industry, industries that at present are buying only about 20 percent of U.S. coal production? The chances of an expanding market here are difficult to predict.

In general, one can divide industries, on the basis of the heat method they use, into boiler industries and process heat industries. Boiler industries use fuel to generate power to run machines that make products. Process industries apply heat generated by fuel to raw materials to make products. The textile industry, for example, is a small boiler industry; the paper and chemical industries are large boiler industries; the food industry is a process heat industry.

Coal can be used as fuel in boilers of all sizes, and experts predict that coal use will increase in the boiler industries. They support this prediction by pointing out that the Powerplant and Industrial Fuel Use Act prohibits the construction of new oil-fired boilers. Laws also require, or reward with tax deductions, the conversion of oil and gas boilers to the use of coal.

In the process heat industries, the heat requirements vary greatly. The baking industry, for example, needs a pollutant-free fuel source that maintains a steady, unvarying temperature. It cannot use coal, for nothing can make coal completely pollutant-free, nor can it be relied upon for a steady level of heat. The glass industry needs a fuel that can build temperatures of 2,500°F in its furnaces, and coal cannot provide temperatures at that level.

It is just not possible to make a flat statement about where coal use is likely to grow outside the boiler industries. Experts seem to think that coal has its best chance of replacing other fuels in the kilns of the cement and lime industries.

The most comprehensive and recent study of the

potential replacement of oil by coal, looking at both the utility industry and "other industries," came up with this specific finding: If all the existing utility and industrial boilers that *can* use coal *did* use coal, and if no new oil or gas-fired boilers are constructed, by 1990 the oil saving would be 2 million barrels per day. To put this number in perspective, utility and large industrial boilers now use about 5.5 million barrels of oil and natural gas each day. It would take about 200 million tons of coal per year, over and above what is now produced, to replace that 2 million barrels per day of oil. Substitution on this scale is the specific goal of the Accelerated Coal Use Program (ACUP), which the President's Commission on Coal proposed in 1980.

Questions were immediately raised, of course, about the environmental impact of this program, and the commission was ready with answers. The program will cause practically no change in the amounts of sulfur dioxide, nitrogen oxides, and particulates in the air, they claim. Coal-fired boilers meeting EPA standards, while burning that amount of coal, would emit fewer pollutants than the oil-burning boilers they would replace.

Continuing their assurances, the commission reported other results of their studies. The buildup of coal use proposed in the ACUP, if carried out without violating the Clean Air Act, would not increase acid rainfall, and CO_2 concentrations would rise by only 0.01 percent.

Critics challenge the claim that increased coal use would be safe for the environment, even under compliance with the Clean Air Act. The act is too lenient, they say. Just the continuation of present levels of pollution, they add, is building up acidity in hundreds of northeastern lakes. These critics take the position that coal-burning factories built before the Clean Air Act must be forced to add scrubbers to *improve* air quality. "Things won't get worse under our program" is no way to defend a program, they maintain. If the program can't promise to make things better, it is not an acceptable program.

Meanwhile, the coal industry is not simply waiting for

the public utility industry to start growing again. It is not waiting for decision makers to recognize low coal prices as a reason to convert to coal. Coal producers are out on the selling trail and finding new markets.

For example, they are selling more coal abroad. In fact, most experts agree that a boom in U.S. coal exports is coming. Like the United States, foreign countries want to be free of dependence upon Middle Eastern oil. They also realize that the Middle East's entire oil supply can last for only a limited time. But, unlike the United States, they do not have vast coal reserves of their own to fall back upon. They are increasingly looking to U.S. coal to supply their present and future energy needs.

A boom in coal exports would benefit the whole nation, not just the coal industry. This is because for many years now, the United States has been troubled by an unfavorable balance of payments. This is the technical term for a fairly simple situation—that U.S. buyers owe foreign sellers more than foreign buyers owe U.S. sellers.

Of course, one of the main reasons for our owing so much money to foreign countries has been the billions of dollars we have been paying each year to import oil. Coal exports could help turn that situation around. Coal sales boosted the "they owe us" figure by $4.5 billion in 1980, and that was a big help in reducing the drain of dollars out of the country.

Finally, there are the "glamour fuels." Will coal find its expanding market and free the United States from foreign oil through the production of coal-based synthetic fuels?

The most knowledgeable responders to these questions say this: Liquefied or gasified coal is not going to have an important place in the energy picture in the next twenty years. Syn-fuel goals have been set and reset in recent years. In July 1979, the federal government announced a program with this goal: 2.5 million barrels per day of oil substitutes by 1990; between 1 and 1.5 million of those barrels were to be coal-based liquids and gases. When the Synthetic Fuels Corporation was established in 1980, 2 million barrels per day was the target figure. A more recent target is 500,000 barrels a day by 1990.

There is much debate over how great a role the government should play in developing syn-fuels. It is most likely that government support will come in the form of guaranteed loans instead of direct grants of money. Companies planning to produce syn-fuels need to borrow large amounts of money to get their plants going. Since nobody can be sure that there really will be a big market for syn-fuels, companies find it hard to borrow. This is where federal "loan guarantees" come in. The federal government guarantees to pay back the loan if the company involved is not able to. This makes borrowing not easy, but easier.

Congress recently authorized $20 billion for loan guarantees to projects for syn-fuels production, with the promise that $68 billion more would come later. Three large syn-fuels projects have actually received guarantees. But to meet even the half-million barrels per day goal, probably ten new plants would have to be built, each of which would cost at least $3 billion. No such number of syn-fuel plants is likely to be on the scene by 1990, for reasons that may be clear from what follows.

It is true that syn-fuels would increase the number of industries in which coal can be of use. Some industrial processes, as we have seen, cannot use coal in conventional ways because the coal cannot produce a hot enough fire or a steady enough heat and because it cannot be a pollutant-free fuel. But some of these processes could use synthetic fuels made from coal.

The technology to produce new coal-based fuels certainly exists. Work on coal liquefaction dates back to the 1930s, when Nazi Germany, rich in coal and poor in oil, turned to research in synthetic fuels. The technology is available to turn coal into fuel oil, gasoline, jet fuel, and diesel oil and to use coal-based liquid fuels as a raw material to produce chemical products.

A relatively low-sulfur fuel called solid solvent refined coal (SRC-I) can be produced from treating pulverized coal at high pressures and temperatures and solidifying the product. Technology exists for producing another product called liquid solvent refined coal (SRC-II) and for producing various coal/oil mixtures.

Producing gas from coal is, of course, not a new idea. During the nineteenth century, the gas lamps that lighted the streets of many cities burned "town gas," a kind of gas with a low heat content that was made from coal. In sharp contrast to this early coal-based gas are the experimental products such as BI-GAS and HYGAS, now being turned out by small, experimental plants. These plants have demonstrated that different kinds of coal can be used to produce different grades of gas and that the best of these grades equals natural gas in every way. Another project, called in-situ gasification, has demonstrated the possibility of burning coal underground in a controlled process that produces a low-Btu gas.

There is no syn-fuels industry in the United States. The Great Plains Gasification Project in North Dakota has its $2 billion loan guarantee; a coal-to-oil plant is operating in Kentucky (other small, experimental plants could be named); and at least a dozen other major enterprises are far along in the planning stage. But there is no established industry.

Ten years ago it was assumed that if the price of oil were to double, syn-fuels could compete with oil. The price of oil has more than quadrupled since then, but it cannot yet be said that syn-fuels can be competitive because we do not yet know how much they will cost. The few experimental projects that have been undertaken have produced such widely different cost figures that nobody is able to quote X dollars per barrel figures at this time. And until a firm figure of this kind is available, it is simply a guess as to whether or not or when synthetic fuel will win a place in the market in competition with oil.

The coal industry spends a substantial amount of money each year keeping track of what it is doing and predicting its own future. Industry reports tell us that well over 800

A coal liquefaction pilot plant under construction.
This plant is expected to be able to process about
600 tons of coal per day, to be made into boiler fuel.

million tons of coal were mined in 1980. Industry projections call for 1.5 billion tons to be mined by 1990. But keep in mind this basic fact: The industry will produce that 1.5 billion tons only if it believes it can sell 1.5 billion tons.

The coal industry has no doubt whatsoever of its ability to meet any production goals that anybody sets for it, any demand that the market creates. But industry confidence and eagerness make up only one side of the coin. Environmentalists and community leaders remind us that licking the air pollution problem associated with coal is only a partial answer to the broad question of whether or not we should look to coal as the short-term answer to the energy problem. They remind us that producing more coal means more deep and surface mining, more community disruption, more safety hazards.

Whether or not these considerations should weigh against the case for increased use of coal is the concern of the chapters that follow.

FIVE

MINING COAL

Around 250 million years ago, swamps filled with large plants covered much of America. As the plants died, they fell into the water, where they were gradually covered by layers of sand and mud. Centuries passed, and the ground slowly shifted above these buried plants, pressing down on them and squeezing out the moisture. The result—coal— looks like hard, black stone. But unlike stone, coal contains the carbon and volatiles that remain from long ago when they were in the living plants. This makes it possible for coal to burn. Thus, it is useful to people.

To get at the coal today, miners must dig down through the layers of dirt and rock that have built up above it. This difficult removal process adds a special complication that makes coal different from other widely used energy sources. There are two basic ways of digging out coal. One is strip mining, which can be used where the coal lies near the surface of the land. The other is underground, or deep, mining. Each poses special problems.

Underground mining has long been used in the coal-producing region of the eastern United States called Appalachia. Surprisingly, even tunneling underneath the earth's surface to get at the coal causes serious hazards to the environment. One of these is damage to underground water supplies. Though all kinds of coal mining endanger underground water, this hazard is most critical in the West. It will be discussed more fully in the section about western mining.

Another environmental hazard of underground mining is the danger of fire. While coal's ability to burn is the reason for its usefulness to people, it also causes one of the great environmental risks of underground mining. Today more than 250 fires are burning out of control through coal seams in America. Some of these fires have continued burning over several years, with no way of putting them out.

Abandoning the mines by no means ends the danger either. For people's homes are on the land's surface, above these raging fires. What does it mean to live above a vast coal fire? Residents of Centralia, Pennsylvania, a town on top of a nineteen-year-long mine fire, explain: "You never know; any day, a house and everybody in it could sink out of sight. That fire down there is burning away the timbers and the columns of coal the miners left to support the roofs of those mine tunnels."

One thirteen-year-old boy narrowly escaped when a 250-foot hole opened up in his grandmother's yard and almost swallowed him. He recalls: "I just grabbed some roots and hung there; the smoke was so thick I couldn't see anything." The smoke pouring out of several holes like these makes the air outside harmful to breathe. And inside several homes, deadly carbon monoxide and carbon dioxide are seeping up through the basements. One resident exclaimed: "My God, what are we to do? You can't live with the windows closed, and you can't stand to have them open."

Angry residents say the federal government's Bureau of Mines is responsible for safety in working and abandoned mines. They feel the government should pay each of them the full value of their homes so they can afford to move away to a safer place. A government spokesman said: "What we're doing is trying to respond to an emergency, and we're giving as fair a price as we can. We had to draw the line somewhere."

People are involved in the actual mining of coal as well. Underground mining is the most dangerous industrial job in America. As the miner descends deeper into the mine pit, the dangers increase. Shut off from the sun's light, the miner works by dim lamplight. Cut off from fresh air, he or she suffocates if an accident breaks the ventilation system. Groundwater might seep through and flood the tunnel. An accidental spark could set off an explosion or a fire. If the roof is not adequately braced, the mine could collapse on the workers.

One miner described every miner's fears: "You are in constant danger at all times in a coal mine. You are surrounded by all the tremendous forces of nature, straining against your effort to extract this coal. So you are in a continual struggle. Nature is out to protect its resources, and you are there wrestling the bowels out of the thing."

Another miner recalled an explosion of methane, a gas that is released as coal is torn from the mine wall: There was no warning—no sight or sound or odor. Suddenly he heard a "boom" and was knocked off his feet by "a rush of air that kept getting stronger and stronger, like a hurricane." It continued nearly half a minute, gagging him with dust. He walked about a thousand feet down the tunnel and found two other dazed miners who had been thrown forty feet by the explosion. "They were breathing heavy, so heavy I could hear them." He continued searching for survivors until the gas became so strong he turned back. Fifteen miners did not walk out of the mine shaft. Each was equipped with a "self-rescuer," a canister containing one to three hours supply of oxygen. Two nights later they were found, dead. This accident occurred in 1981.

Over 100,000 U.S. miners have died in mine accidents in this century. Hundreds of thousands more have "black lung" disease from long years of working in mines.

Conditions have improved since coal's early days, but safety remains a bitterly controversial issue. One writer states: "The mine operators have traditionally fought the added expense of greater safety measures as a threat to their production and profits." Critics charge that, to the operators, "men are cheaper than coal."

Despite the resistance of mine owners, the Federal Coal Mine Health and Safety Act became law in 1970. In 1981, the Supreme Court ruled that mine safety inspectors could make surprise inspections of mines to be sure that safety rules were being obeyed.

A recent study of mine safety showed that fatal mine accidents have sharply declined. It also showed a dramatic difference in the safety records of different mining companies; the company with the best record had seven times fewer accidents than the company with the worst record. In other words, it can be done; mines can be made safer. Today, owners and miners increasingly agree about the need to invest in mine safety, but for different reasons. One coal industrialist explained the mine owners' point of view: "There is no longer any question that a safer mine is a more productive mine."

The need to increase mine productivity, the amount of coal produced by each worker, has become increasingly important in the coal industry. After World War II, coal's importance rapidly fell with competition from oil and natural gas. Coal mine owners tried to protect their profits by paying as little as possible for the labor needed to produce each ton of coal. Their solution was to mechanize the mines. This meant that instead of paying five miners to produce one ton of coal, they would pay one miner using a modern machine to produce that ton of coal.

Mechanizing the mines became a controversial issue itself. John L. Lewis, leader of the UMW, believed that mechanization was necessary to save the coal industry. He stated: "We have encouraged the leading companies in the coal industry to resort to mechanization in order to increase the living standards of the miner and to improve his working conditions." And it did—for the miners who kept their jobs. But, of course, many miners opposed mechanization because it forced them from their jobs. Especially in the eastern mining region of Appalachia, deep poverty struck unemployed miners who were no longer able to earn a living.

Mechanization was still a key issue in the most recent UMW strike of 1981. By this time, modern mines had workers operating extremely expensive "longwall" mechanical miners that ripped out the coal, then automatically carried it off on a conveyor. These machines were so expensive that mine owners wanted them to be in use twenty-four hours a day, seven days a week. But many miners refused to work on Sundays.

This was only one issue in the coal strike of 1981. Many miners believed they were striking to save their once-powerful union. At the height of the UMW's power, practically all coal mined in the United States was mined by UMW members; by 1981 only 44 percent of U.S. coal was mined by UMW miners. But coal producers were required to pay a fee to the UMW for each ton of coal mined by nonunion miners. And they were required to use union miners in certain areas. In the 1981 contract, the owners tried to drop these two requirements. But the majority of union members felt this would destroy their union by freeing owners to increasingly employ nonunion miners. So the UMW went on strike.

Mining coal, then, is much more than a mechanical process like piping oil or gas out of the ground. It depends upon a labor force with a stormy history. This labor situation adds uncertainty to the coal industry's present situation. Customers who are considering investing in coal hesitate because they fear that their fuel supply might well be interrupted by a coal miners' strike. This has been a major barrier to the coal industry's ability to win long-term contracts from foreign countries that are interested in buying coal.

In 1981, leaders in the coal industry realized that they were losing money because possible customers were concerned about U.S. coal's labor problems. They remembered losing major contracts during the last coal strike, which had occurred in 1978 and had lasted 111 days. All this put pressure on the mine owners to quickly come to an agreement with the miners in 1981. Though the strike of 1981 did not

Coal Areas of the United States

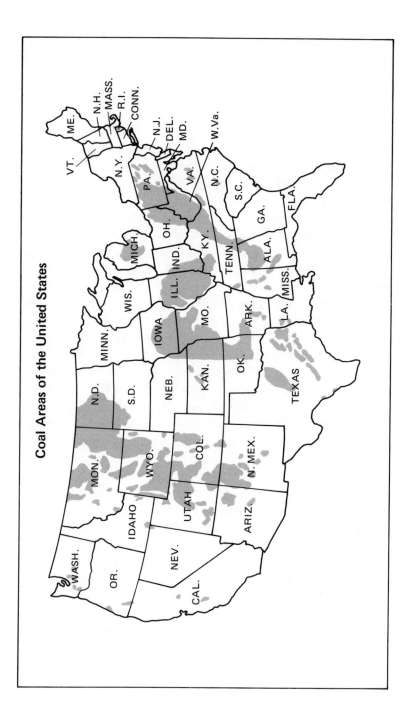

cause a national emergency, as did earlier UMW strikes, the mine owners gave in to many of the miners' demands. They wanted a settlement that would show buyers that the U.S. coal industry had a "stable" labor force that was back on the job with a secure contract. On the other hand, UMW members also knew in 1981 that there might be a great increase in coal sales. They believed that if they did not insist on their demands, the miners' union would be shut out of the profits from the coming coal boom.

Today's energy crisis has indeed opened up great possibilities for growth of coal's markets. One result is that mines are being developed in the western United States to produce coal that once was not considered worth mining. Long ago, when the shifting surface of the earth was pressing the moisture out of coal, this pressure was not the same in all places. In general, more moisture remained in coal in the western United States than in coal in the East. A chunk of eastern coal produces more heat per pound (higher rank) than a similar chunk of many western coals. Thus, it burns with a hotter flame. With our increased need for energy, there is now a market for burning lower-ranking western coal.

The Clean Air legislation of the 1970s also added to demand for western coal. For, in addition to containing less carbon, western coal also generally contains less sulfur than eastern coal. Sulfur dioxide, you'll recall, is a major pollutant from burning coal. Coal-burning plants can often avoid the great expense of adding scrubbers to control sulfur dioxide emissions just by switching to low-sulfur western coal.

Much of western coal lies within 200 feet of the present surface of the land. This makes it possible to use a more efficient removal process than underground mining, which can recover only about 50 to 60 percent of the coal seam. Most shallow western coal deposits can be removed by surface, or strip, mining, which recovers up to 90 percent of the coal seam.

Instead of tunneling down through the hundreds of tons

of rock and dirt that have formed over the coal seam, surface mining strips away the layers of dirt and rock. Sometimes these layers, called overburden, are removed with ordinary bulldozers. But increasingly, overburden is removed by gigantic power shovels that are as tall as a twenty-story building and can pick up enough material to fill three railroad cars. In this way, the coal seam is exposed and can be broken up and hauled away.

In many cases, the strip mining process used to end at this point. Once the coal was removed, the mine was abandoned. In hours, the result of centuries of gradual change and growth were undone.

But the days of abandoning strip-mined land are over. An important step, reclamation, must now follow coal removal in every strip mine in the United States. This means that after the coal has been hauled away, the overburden must be replaced and trees, bushes, or grasses must be planted. As far as possible, the land must be returned to its former state, for in 1977, after a nine-year battle between environmentalists and coal producers, the Surface Mining Control and Reclamation Act (SMCRA) became law.

SMCRA did not introduce reclamation to U.S. strip mining. Several states already had strict reclamation requirements controlling mining within their borders. But other states had no requirements at all. Before 1977, about 4 million acres of U.S. land had been affected by strip mining. Forty-three percent of these acres had been damaged by mining. Half the 1.3 million acres of strip-mined land in the East had not been reclaimed. SMCRA brought uniform reclamation requirements to all U.S. strip mining.

It may seem strange for coal producers to have battled with environmentalists to avoid dumping dirt back in a hole and planting vegetation on top. Of course it was not really as simple as that. The aim of the SMCRA was to protect the environment from the many hazards that go along with tearing open a huge piece of land and removing a large quantity of coal that had been part of that land for millions of years. Understanding some of the complexities involved

Strip mining coal by dragline.

Strip mining coal by power shovel.

in trying to meet this goal may explain why coal producers were reluctant to take on such an expensive and difficult responsibility.

Land that has been successfully reclaimed must meet these three requirements:

- It must resist erosion. That is, it must be covered with plants that grip the soil so they do not wash away in heavy rains.

- These plants must be able to survive with no outside help, such as irrigation or fertilization.

- The land must have at least the same productivity it had before mining. For example, land that had been used for grazing animals must be able to provide food and water for animals again after mining.

These requirements are necessary because land that contains coal is usually vitally important to the nation for other reasons as well. For example, coal seams that could help free us from dependence upon Middle Eastern oil often lie under land that is providing our food supply. The basis for controversy here is clear. Which is more important, mining coal or growing food? Reclamation holds out the hope that such difficult choices will not have to be made.

Successful reclamation requires controlling the damage done under the ground as well as planting over the huge scar that strip mining leaves on the land's surface. This is because mining coal is intricately tied up with a far more precious natural resource, our underground supply of water.

It is possible for water to pass through coal. In fact, coal seams provide part of a vast, natural, underground system of pathways for water as it seeps down from the ground's surface after rainfalls. These underground pathways for water are called aquifers. This close relationship between coal and underground water helps explain why flooding was a hazard in coal mining before powered pumps were invented. Aquifers are important, not just because they provide water's underground transportation system, but because they filter impurities out of the water as it passes through.

Tearing out a coal seam, then, endangers the land's, and people's, water supply in different ways. First, of course, it destroys water's underground transportation routes. Water that once filtered down to a certain underground pool might no longer end up there. People who have sunk wells to tap that water supply may find that their wells have gone dry. The aquifer's natural filtering process is also lost. Furthermore, the dirt and minerals that are jarred loose by mining can be picked up by underground water. Thus, the water may remain, but its purity may be destroyed.

The effects of mining upon water are especially serious in the West because there is far less rainfall there than in the East. Even without the extra burden of strip mining, shortages of water are often there a problem.

The SMCRA attempts to limit the damage strip mining does when it upsets a complex natural pattern. The Office of Surface Mining (OSM) was created to carry out this goal. The coal producer, hoping to open up an area for surface mining, must deal with a mass of OSM regulations and inspections. This is similar to the complicated process the industrialist must go through to meet EPA regulations before constructing a new factory. Before mining can begin, an application permit must be filed. Words like "voluminous" and "encyclopedic" are used to describe this application permit. It must contain the results of a detailed study of all aspects of the area's natural environment, the specific plan for mining the land, and the exact proposed method for reclaiming that particular area. Many experts are called in to judge the permit application. A Final Environmental Impact Statement is issued. At last, a decision is made on whether the environmental risk is too great or whether the coal producer can proceed with the mine.

The coal producer is by no means free to proceed,

even after this long application process. Before beginning, a "performance bond" must be paid to cover the full costs of reclamation in case the company fails to successfully reclaim the land. "Success" is determined only if the new vegetation is doing well after ten years with no outside help and the land's renewed productivity has been proven. From the beginning of the mining process to the end of this period, OSM inspectors check to be sure the mine operator is living up to all points in the detailed mining and reclamation plans.

In light of all this delay, expense, and extra responsibility, the mine owners' reason for fighting passage of the SMCRA was understandable. To them SMCRA was part of the "coal nightmare" of regulations that have blocked development of their industry at every step. On the other hand, an independent study of the effects of the SMCRA has concluded that "contrary to industry forecasts when the law was passed, coal production has not been stifled" by the need to reclaim mined land. It also notes that having uniform regulation requirements throughout the nation is fairer to the entire coal industry. Coal producers in states with strict reclamation laws no longer have to compete with producers who do not have to bother with land reclamation.

But the fight against SMCRA continues. After 1977, the coal industry tried to have the new law declared unconstitutional. This effort was defeated by the Supreme Court in 1981. More recently, coal producers have tried to dull the effect of the law by reducing the inspection power of the OSM.

At the same time, a different attitude is also growing in the coal industry, especially in the newer mining regions of the West. Coal producers are beginning to believe that it is in their own best interests to do as little harm as possible to the area they are mining. Community resentment, they have found, can be as powerful a barrier to the coal industry's development as federal regulations.

The opening of a new mine does more than upset the

natural environment. It also produces a "boom town" in the area of the mine. The opportunity for employment attracts many new workers and their families. The community cannot take care of all these new people. Sewers back up, water supplies run short, homes and schools are crowded. "That's not our problem," the coal producers might say.

But, because coal mining depends heavily upon its labor force, it is their problem. The community resents the mine that has disrupted its life. The workers are part of the community. Studies have shown that resentful workers frequently fail to show up for work. Or they quit altogether, forcing the employers to waste time hiring and training new workers. And they do not work as hard as happy workers. In other words, mine productivity suffers.

Productivity continues to be a serious problem in the coal industry, even with mechanization. There are many possible explanations for this. But studies generally show that mines providing the best living and working conditions for their workers have high productivity.

Communities in coal-rich areas are not waiting for concern over mine productivity to cause coal operators to do something about the boom towns they may create. Many local governments in these areas will not allow mining to begin on their land until mine owners agree to help the community provide for the rush of new people who will be moving there. So, increasingly, mine operators are contributing to enlarging schools and building housing in areas they plan to mine. One politician summed up the changing attitude of mine operators when he said, "Industry has learned some hard lessons. Fact is, we had to beat some of those lessons into them with two by fours."

The effects of the industry's changing attitude can be seen in the contrast between the old mining areas of the East and the new mining areas of the West, where most of these changes have taken place. For example, the coal strike of 1981 was not just a rivalry between miners and owners. It was also a clash between eastern and western miners. The overwhelming majority of western UMW mem-

bers voted to accept the contract that had been nego-
tiated by their leaders and the mine owners. It was the eastern miners who rejected the contract and caused the
strike. Bitter western UMW members were forced to go
along with the strike and stop working. One western miner
noted, "In Appalachia there is a lot of tradition based on
the memory of things gone by." Another said that "the
resentment in Appalachia is that, no matter what happens,
they think they are being had by the companies."

These western miners believe that eastern miners are
destroying the UMW rather than saving it. One of the biggest threats to union miners is competition for jobs from
nonunion miners. In fact, union miners once used violence
to force other miners to join their union. But many western
miners do not want to join a union that is dominated by the
"strike happy" eastern miners. One western miner summed
up this point of view by asking, "Why would anyone who
wants steady work want to join an outfit like this?"

Western mining is increasing its role in the U.S. coal
industry. This is the area where the growth in mining will cen-
ter—if growth in consumption really comes about. This will
cause another problem for the coal industry. For the West is
not prepared to transport all this new coal.

SIX

MOVING COAL

Very little coal is used right where it is mined. Slightly under two-thirds of it leaves the mines by railroad. Barges and trucks divide two-thirds of the balance of the coal fairly evenly between them. Conveyor belts and short-haul trucks carry a little over 11 percent to public utility plants that are close enough to the mine to be called "mine-mouth" plants.

The coal that moves by railroad can be transported no other way, so the health of the coal industry is tied very closely to the state of the railroads. Furthermore, this tie between railroads and coal will probably become even stronger in the years ahead.

Railroad coal traffic—tons carried and miles covered— is expected to rise more sharply in the 1980s than coal use. This is because more western (west of the Mississippi River) coal will probably enter the market. You will recall that the coal industry predicts that 1.5 billion tons of coal will be mined per year by 1990. They also predict that almost half of that coal may be drawn from western coal mines. This would be a dramatic shift in eastern versus western coal production.

Two comparisons between eastern and western coal offer some support for the idea that the shift will indeed take place. At the present time, about 80 percent of the

Moving coal by train.

coal that is mined in the United States comes from fields east of the Mississippi River. But the reserves of the East are only 45 percent of the nation's total coal reserves. So western reserves will have to be drawn upon more heavily if coal use goes up as expected.

The second point was mentioned in the last chapter, the difference between the coal of the two regions in sulfur content and Btu rating. Businessmen will think about their pollution-control costs and heating-power needs in deciding whether to buy eastern or western coal. But growth in western coal use can nonetheless be predicted with confidence. And that means that moving coal will need increasing attention.

Railroads will need large quantities of new equipment. Rail roadbeds, miles upon miles of which have fallen into disrepair, will have to be fixed up and maintained.

A government study was launched in 1977 to answer this question: Can the country's transportation system move fuels from where they are found or processed to the places where they are to be used? The part of the study dealing with railroads concluded that the railroads would be able to play their part.

Railroads, they concluded, would have no difficulty borrowing the money needed to do track work and buy cars. The manufacturers of coal cars reported that they could easily fill any orders for new equipment that came their way.

But not everyone agrees that raising the necessary funds for railroad expansion will present no problems. On the contrary, railroad expansion raises the whole question of railroad rates. Some say that railroad rates must rise. They must be high enough, it is claimed, so that railroads can provide the additional services that will be needed if more coal is to be moved. Others say that railroad rates must be kept down so that coal can be moved yet remain competitive with other fuels in price. What actually is going on in regard to railroad rates and coal will be considered shortly.

But before that, another point concerning rail traffic must be considered.

More than money is involved in railroad transportation. About half the coal hauled by the railroads moves on "unit trains" made up of a hundred or more cars. These cars are never uncoupled. They move almost like a conveyor belt between mines and generating plants, taking on coal as they move, slowing down to dump the coal, stopping only to change crews. If expanding coal traffic brought forty-eight such trains through your town each day, might you have second thoughts about whether the country should use more coal?

In the city of Littleton, Colorado, for example, a few years ago, neighborhood after neighborhood was the scene of a morning coffee hour, or some other get-together, in which the topic of discussion was the building of a trench. No, the city wasn't about to engage in trench warfare. It wanted to put the railroad track that runs through the city under street level.

With thirty-five trains, often a mile long, moving through the community each day—and facing the possibility that this number might be doubled by 1990—community leaders felt that it was urgent for Littleton residents to vote in favor of a tax proposal that would raise local taxes to pay its share of a federal-state-county-city railroad venture that would cost over $20 million. Nobody likes higher taxes, but it was clear that the city was being seriously affected by the noise and the traffic congestion every time one of those trains passed. Not even fire-fighting equipment could move freely.

Littleton's problem arose out of the boom in Wyoming coal. This boom caused a vast increase in railroad traffic in the rail corridor that runs along the eastern slope of the Rockies, linking the coal fields of Wyoming and the power plants of Texas and Oklahoma that depend upon these fields for their fuel.

There may be another solution to Littleton's problem

and the problem of other communities where railroad traffic is disrupting everyday life. The point was made above that the coal that is hauled by rail can travel only that way. That is not really true. There is another way to move coal long distances. The technology exists to reduce coal to a powder, mix it with water, and send it through a pipeline to its destination. There, the water can be removed to make the coal ready for use.

There is nothing new about these so-called "slurry pipelines." The first patent for the process was issued in 1891, and a slurry pipeline was carrying coal into London in 1914. But in the United States, slurry pipelines have run into many obstacles. Any project that uses water, as these pipelines do, is looked upon with suspicion in the water-hungry West. And any coal-moving enterprise that needs right of way across land owned by railroads finds the railroads bitterly opposed to granting that right of way. Laws have actually been introduced in Congress that would force the railroads to yield a bit on this subject, but the railroads' friends in Congress have kept such laws from going through.

It is easy to understand why railroads fight rivals for the coal-carrying business. One-third of all the money the railroads take in as freight charges comes from carrying coal.

One would think that because coal means money to the railroads that the health of the coal industry would be of vital importance to the railroads. The railroads, in fact, loudly proclaim that this is indeed the case. But from the point of view of many coal producers, the railroads do not always do what is best for coal's health.

Earlier in this book, we said that the delivered price of coal currently varies, from place to place, from one-fifth to one-half the price of a comparable amount of oil. The point of the comparison given was the difference between the price of coal and the price of oil. However, here we are more concerned with the part of the statement that says, "varies from place to place." This means that the same ton of coal can cost twice as much in one place as it does in another. The explanation for that difference lies almost entirely in the cost of transportation, which the coal buyer finds added to the bill.

Railroad rates are regulated by the Interstate Commerce Commission (ICC), which has a twofold responsibility. It must protect shippers against unfair rates, but it must also try to improve the condition of the railroad system as a whole—to "revitalize the railroads." To accomplish the second purpose, the ICC can give more favorable rates to one kind of cargo than to another. It can also permit freight rates that favor one part of the country over another.

The ICC has taken the position that freight charges for coal, especially in the West, may be higher than the cost of moving the coal (107 percent of the cost, to be exact). The ICC defends this decision with this line of reasoning: If coal more than pays its way on the railroads, other kinds of freight can be allowed to move at less than what they cost. The less-than-cost rates go to shippers who can, if they choose, use another means of transportation. This keeps them railroad customers. More-than-cost rates, on the other hand, do not drive the coal business away because there is no place for it to go.

Coal freight rates produce some strange results. There are places where the freight cost per ton of coal is greater than the mine-mouth cost per ton. There are cities near the coastlines of the United States where it is cheaper for a coal-using industry to buy its fuel from an overseas coal company and pay the freight bill for shipping rather than the railroad freight bill for U.S. coal.

Railroad freight rates can have another harmful effect on the coal industry. They can drive away potential coal industry customers. Fuel cost, you will remember, is a crucial factor when, say, a public utility generating plant is making a decision on the question of whether to get rid of an oil-fired boiler and install in its place a coal-fired boiler, plus add all the pollution-control equipment that is required to meet the community's air standards. High freight rates for coal added to the mine-mouth price of the coal may add up to a delivered price that makes the decision come out no—it will stay with oil.

You saw in an earlier chapter that coal exports explain some of the coal industry's recent growth. This export business has created, however, serious transportation problems. More exports of coal mean the need for more ships to carry it; more ships mean the need for ports that can dock them, load them, and get them on their way, all in short order.

The officer of a European coal-buying association put this very bluntly to an audience of U.S. coal producers who were seeking advice on how to build up their overseas markets. "Gentlemen," she said, "until you get it out of the country, you haven't sold it."

There is nothing strange in a German industrialist, for example, asking questions about an American port. He knows that the coal he is ordering will be shipped to him from that port. So he asks: Is the port deep enough to handle a large coal carrier? Is the moving and loading equipment at the piers the most efficient type? He investigates because anything less than top efficiency costs him money.

Shipping his entire order in one big carrier will cost him less than if the order travels in two smaller ships. If a ship booked to carry his order sits at anchor at a port, waiting its turn to be loaded, costs of between $15,000 and $18,000 a day accumulate on his bill.

The United States was simply not ready for a surge of coal exports. Until recently it was the only major coal-exporting country that had no ports that could handle the so-called super-colliers—freighters that can carry 150,000 tons of coal, some even more. Serious delays have developed at several U.S. coal ports. At Hampton Roads, Virginia, for example, the largest coal port in the United States, ships have at times had to wait for months to be loaded.

Since the early 1980s, there has been a flurry of activity to deal with the problem of coal-port congestion. Federal laws now permit harbor dredging at Hampton Roads, Virginia; New Orleans/Baton Rouge, Louisiana; and Mobile, Alabama; these ports can now accommodate super-colliers. Dozens of projects are under construction or in the planning stage that will increase coal handling capacity in ports on both the East and West coasts.

These projects are being carried on in a number of different ways. Coal companies are doing some of the port expansion work; railroads are doing some of it. A city government may improve its own port or cooperate with another city or a state government to get port improvement under way.

One U.S. coal company, for example, which succeeded in getting a long-term contract to supply coal to a Japanese firm, is cooperating with three other coal companies to develop a coal export terminal at Newport News, Virginia. The contract it made with the Japanese company says that if there are any demurrage (waiting-to-be-shipped) charges such as those referred to above, the Japanese company does not have to pay them. The coal company pays. It is easy to see why that U.S. coal supplier is taking steps to insure that the fuel going to its Japanese customer will have no shipping delays.

Some observers think it is unfortunate that there is rivalry among railroads, coal companies, and shipyards, for the business of handling coal in port. Some think there will be an overcapacity—too many coal loading ports for the amount of coal to be shipped—in the not too distant future.

This view of the coal export business prompted one writer to describe it as a chicken-and-egg situation. The foreign buyers want to see the ports in place, the railroads in place, and the mines in place before they sign large contracts. The coal producer wants the contract so he or she can finance the mines.

This statement reflects the fear that timing may cause problems. But timing problems or no, the nation's transportation system can probably be fixed and expanded to meet the needs of an expanding coal industry. Whether or not there will be equal success in working out fairly the issue of railroad rates for coal and wise solutions to the community problems caused by increased railroad traffic, it is far too early to tell.

SEVEN

WHAT FUTURE FOR COAL?

The meeting that had just begun had attracted an attentive and interested audience that filled the room. The chairman had emphasized in his opening remarks that the speakers wanted an informal meeting. Questions, they had agreed, would be welcomed at any point in their talks. So no one was disturbed when the first speaker was interrupted at the end of his first sentence. This is the exchange that took place:

> *Speaker:* We are here to figure out how to use coal without damaging the environment.
> *Member of audience:* Sir, would you repeat what you just said?
> *Speaker:* Of course. I said, "We are here to figure out how to use coal without damaging the environment."
> *Member of audience:* Thank you. I never before heard anybody from industry express concern about the environment. I wanted to be sure I heard you correctly.

A strange exchange? Not really, under the circumstances. An exchange very like this actually took place during a meeting of the National Coal Policy Project. This was a series of meetings, held in the year 1978, in which leading environmentalists met face to face with top and middle-rank officers of coal mining companies and companies in the coal-using industries. Nothing like this project had ever happened before in the coal industry, and the most amazing thing about it was the change that took place in the people who were part of the project. They moved, over the months, from the suspicion suggested above to respect for each other, and to agreement on a wide number of subjects.

Of course, some environmentalists outside the project were outraged at the notion that fellow environmentalists would yield on anything; some industry diehards charged "sellout" to "those hold-back-progress freaks."

Why the meeting? Why the antagonism? Why the conflict of interests? Let us be very clear about this. There *is* a built-in conflict between these two stated U.S. policy goals:

(1) Use more coal to reduce dependence
    upon imported oil.
(2) Clean up the nation's air, water, and land.

Examples of this conflict, and approaches that have been tried to settle some of the issues, have been offered all through this book.

The purpose of this final chapter is to look at the conflict from a broader point of view, to present some approaches to working out the conflict that have not yet been touched upon; to present two anticoal charges; and to end with some changes within the coal industry that are likely to be significant in the months and years ahead.

The slow pace at which boilers are being converted from oil to coal has caused some observers to say that the process would get on much faster if both industry and environmentalists would give a little. To get some feeling of what "give a little" might mean, consider what came out of the Coal Policy Project.

For the first time, industry representatives agreed to the

principle that certain areas should be "off limits" to mining—national parks, for example, or areas where mining might threaten the water supply. In return for this came concessions on reclamation of the land after strip mining. Environmentalists came around to admitting that maybe industry has a point when it says that it should not have to level the great piles of material dug from the earth in strip mining. Maybe we should at least consider the suggestion that some places be left high and the rest really be leveled. It might be better than the slope that sometimes results when the entire area is leveled.

Industry accepted the idea that when a mining company begins to think about Place X as a site for future operations, it should give the people of Place X ample prior notice, preferably during the planning stage. It should not just spring the project on them at the stage of filing permission requests.

Environmentalists, in return, made a concession on one of the points that bothers industry most—delaying tactics. The envrionmentalists readily admitted that they often employ such tactics. If the regulations say that the people of a community may ask for a chance to hear a mining company's plans, they will insist that there be a meeting for that purpose, they said. So the mining company may find itself in first this public hearing, then that public hearing, then another public hearing, and so on.

As industry people talked face to face with representatives of groups that had often been responsible for delays, they came to realize that the environmentalists often used delaying tactics because they did not have the money to hire experts or attorneys to fight industry on matters of fact. A company expert might say that digging at a certain site will have no effect upon the underground water supply. The local group was unlikely to have their own expert who could contradict this statement. Delay was often their only weapon.

So industry accepted the principle of public support for public interest groups, and the environmentalists accepted the principle that there should be *one* hearing and *one* impact study instead of the repetition and overlapping and duplication that often now prevails.

One lesson can certainly be drawn from the National Coal Policy Project—the possibilities that open up when people on opposite sides of an issue exchange ideas instead of exchanging charges and insults.

There has been no revolution at the EPA since 1978. No claim has been made that the trends talked about below are an outgrowth of the project. But new approaches are evolving; compromises are being made. Those who like these new approaches call the compromises a spirit of flexibility and commend the EPA for that flexibility. Those who object call the changes a sellout to antienvironmentalists.

Here are some examples. Take the situation of a city that does not meet Clean Air standards. Under a letter-of-the-law enforcement of the Clean Air Act, no new industry would be permitted in that city that would produce any pollution.

Now the EPA is, in some cases, permitting "offsets." An industry causing X amount of new pollution will be permitted in City A if it is offset by a reduction in pollution, equal to or greater than X, by other plants in City A.

The pollution-reducing plants may be owned by the same company that wants to bring in the new plant. Or, the new company may buy the offsets from other companies. For example, a major oil company received permission to build an oil terminal by paying for pollution-control equipment at three dry-cleaning plants and a power station.

Critics refer to offsets as "buying the right to pollute the air"; supporters defend the offset approach as a way of controlling pollution and yet permitting new enterprises.

Here is another closely related example of what some call flexibility, others call sellout. According to the letter of the Clean Air regulations, the emissions from each smokestack on a plant must be monitored. No stack may emit more than, say, 5 units of pollutants per day. At Plant A, with five stacks, Stack 1 emits 10 units of pollutant each day;

Stack 2 emits 8 units; Stack 3 emits 5 units; Stacks 4 and 5 emit 1 unit each per day. Under the letter of the law, the company would be required to do something about Stacks 1 and 2.

But in some cases industry has proposed, and the EPA has gone along with, what is called the "bubble" approach. Under the bubble principle, a plant is handled as if it were operating under a huge bubble. All the pollutant-emitting parts of the plant are treated as one unit. With five stacks, the limit is 25 units of pollutants. In Plant A, 10 plus 8 plus 5 plus 1 plus 1 equal 25. Plant A does not need to install any pollution controls; it enjoys a substantial saving in cost.

In the framing of pollution-control laws, cost is an idea that is rejected by many environmentalists. Their position is that the only way to clean up air, water, or land is to follow three principles: (1) set specific standards that reflect what is necessary or desirable for public health and welfare and rigid timetables for the achievement of those standards; (2) in setting these standards, do not take into consideration the cost of compliance with the standards; make health and welfare the criteria, not cost; and (3) enforce the standards to the letter.

In contrast to this, a major change sought by many critics of the Clean Air Act is that laws should take cost into consideration. Right now, plants in every pollutant-creating industry in a given area must reduce their emissions to the same standard. In Industry A, it would cost, say, $100,000 per year to meet the standard; in Industry B, it would cost $500,000 to reduce pollutant X to the same standard. Critics of the Clean Air Act say to concentrate on Industry A. Clean up the industry in which it will cost least to meet standards. The end result will be cleaner air and a lower burden of cost on industry as a whole. And that cost burden is important to all of us, the critics maintain, because the costs of pollution control are passed along in the higher prices that contribute to inflation.

The EPA does sometimes permit a company to use cost

as an argument for taking Step A instead of Step B in order to carry out an EPA order to reduce its emission of a certain pollutant. For example, a steel company was ordered to reduce the emission of particulates from an open-hearth furnace. After making a study of all its dust-creating activities, the company found that more dust was coming from piles of iron ore stored in its yards than from its furnace. All it had to do was spray water on the piles of iron ore, a very inexpensive operation, and dust emissions were reduced more than if the company had installed costly pollution-control equipment in the furnace. The EPA permitted this form of compliance in this particular case and has made a few similar rulings in other situations.

We now must turn to a totally different point of view about coal and energy policy for the near and more distant future. We must look at the position of those who say that coal is not the major alternative to imported oil, not a bridge to an energy-rich future. The only alternative, some say, must be conservation. Don't encourage investment of large sums to increase the conventional use of coal. Instead, put coal in the long-range picture. Whatever attention is given to coal now should focus on more intensive coal research—further research into methods of burning coal cleanly and further research into conversion of coal to liquid or gas.

A striking example of the effectiveness of conservation was given in Chapter One, so the enthusiasm for it is easy to understand. Conservationists prefer to speak of conservation not as a way of saving energy but rather as a source of energy. Saving energy suggests that we will refrain from making X and thereby save the energy that would have been used in the making. Source of energy, the proponents of this view feel, emphasizes a better approach. We can make X, but make it using the energy-efficient techniques that conservation studies have taught us to employ. Conservationists, in other words, prefer to avoid the notions of sacrifice and self-denial—of doing without. They prefer to stress instead adjustment of present ways of doing things to more energy-efficient ways of doing things.

It is beyond the scope of this book to go into great detail about the possibilities and problems involved in embarking on a commitment to conservation as a major source of energy. But two examples of "adjustment" are offered below.

About one-third of all the miles driven in the United States in the course of a year are in trips to and from the place of work. One study has found that about 50 million Americans are alone in their cars as they make these trips. If each carried one passenger—which means 25 million instead of 50 million round trips daily—we are told that 400,000 barrels of oil per day would be saved. And not one cent of additional investment would be needed. Some doubling up in driving to work contributed to the conservation results given in Chapter One.

To put that figure, 400,000 barrels, into perspective, remember that the goal of the whole Accelerated Coal Use Program of 1980 was to save 2 million barrels of oil per day, and that goal, as we have seen, involves major changes and investments.

Walk along the streets of midtown New York City on a cold winter day, and you may occasionally see steam rising through holes in the pavement. This means that "cogeneration" is going on in New York City. Con Edison, which supplies the city with electricity, sells the steam left over from producing that electricity to about two thousand office and apartment buildings—steam heat. Cogeneration, in other words, is the combined production of electricity and heat. Cogeneration is conservation. Cogeneration reduces fuel use.

When electricity is produced separately, the steam heat given off by the power plant is wasted. Perhaps as much as two-thirds of the fuel's Btu's are lost in this way. With cogeneration, the steam is piped to places where heat is needed for an industrial process or simply to keep homes or industrial areas warm.

When an industrial plant uses fuel at very high temperatures to create steam, steam which it then proceeds to use at much lower temperatures, much heat is wasted. With cogeneration, that excess temperature is used to drive a turbine, thus producing electricity as a by-product.

Moving toward cogeneration in industry would be another example of going back to an energy practice of another day. Many companies in the early 1900s did produce their own electricity as a by-product of producing the steam to run their plants. Most gave it up when electric power from utility plants became very inexpensive. Also, they did not wish to be classified as public utilities and come under the regulations that control that line of business.

Controversy rages over what percentage of U.S. energy needs can be met by conservation and over how soon that contribution could be felt. One highly respected recent study said that conservation could, but very probably would not, supply as much as 40 percent.

There is fairly strong support for the estimate that conservation could supply 29 to 30 percent of our energy needs, but not very quickly. The first 10 to 15 percent, it is claimed, could come easily through better insulation, better maintenance of furnaces, more economical heating and cooling practices, and the like.

Beyond these simple, so-called housekeeping measures would have to come changes that require spending large sums of money, and that will take time. The point is made that it takes twenty to thirty years to "turn over" the nation's housing stock, and ten years to "turn over" the automobile fleet. An energy-efficient house for every family and an energy-efficient car for every driver—these goals are not going to be met in a hurry.

Industry has really achieved a better conservation record than consumers in recent years. Great progress has been made in using energy-efficient methods of producing goods. In fact, the figures show that the amount of energy used per unit of goods produced has gone down in the last few years.

The second major anticoal position is not a preference for an alternative energy source but rather a pessimistic view of the coal industry itself. The argument runs like this: The coal industry is so troubled by poor management, so burdened with labor unrest, that it cannot transform itself into the stable, technologically advanced industry that could produce, reliably, year after year, almost twice the coal it is producing now.

Much evidence has been offered in the preceding chapters that supports or contradicts this opinion. Here are some broader ideas to bring to bear upon the state of the coal industry.

First, significant changes are taking place in ownership and management of the coal industry. Up until fairly recently, most coal mining was carried on by individual coal companies. A few steel companies owned mines, as did a few public utilities. Then, in the 1960s, oil companies began to enter the picture. Of the twenty-five largest oil corporations, seventeen were in the coal business by the mid-1970s, either by buying up existing coal mining companies or by forming new companies to mine lands acquired by the parent oil companies. The number of utility companies among the major coal-producing units also has increased, and companies whose business is the development of new technologies of coal conversion are getting into the mining of coal.

Some concern has been expressed that the entrance of oil producers into the coal industry will reduce the competition that has normally prevailed between oil and coal. But several independent studies suggest otherwise. There is still healthy competition in coal. It is not an industry in which a small number of firms control half or more of the industry.

The new people in the coal business are able, experienced business people. Some are ready to try new ideas, like the ones described in Chapter Five. They are installing new equipment. Many of them are very safety-minded, and accidents, it has been pointed out, are down. In many mines a more competent level of supervisor works with the miners right at the mine level. Safety committees chosen by the workers themselves are given the time and freedom to check up on safety equipment and safety practices in the mine.

Second, the labor picture in the industry has changed. The changed attitude toward the once all-powerful UMW has been noted, and interesting developments are taking place in the nonunion mines. Wages there are high and fringe benefits—insurance, days off, and the like—are excellent. In fact, in recent years, what nonunion workers were given has set the standard that union negotiators then went out to get. The significance of new labor and management attitudes as shown in the settlement of the 1981 strike has already been emphasized.

In other words, many would say that a stable, technologically advanced industry seems to be appearing.

No one who speaks or writes on energy, no matter what his or her enthusiasm for any energy source other than coal, denies that coal has a place—an important place—in our energy future. What, then, is the coal question? Three questions were raised early in this book: *Can* coal, *should* coal, and *will* coal be important in the bridge years and in the new era some hundred years away?

Perhaps *can* coal was never a question. The figures concerning coal are the answer. Perhaps *should* coal is less debatable than we had thought. Maybe the real coal question is, will the chain of decisions needed to put coal to work reliably, on an adequate scale, and in acceptable ways, be made all along the line by small businesses, by large businesses, by giant utilities, by railroads, by shipping lines, by government, and by the coal mining companies— *and will these decisions be made in time?*

SUGGESTED READINGS

Branley, Franklyn M. *Energy for the Twenty-first Century.* New York: Thomas Y. Crowell, 1975.

Chaffin, Lillie D. *Coal: Energy and Crisis.* New York: Harvey House, 1974.

Coombs, Charles. *Coal in the Energy Crisis.* New York: William Morrow, 1980.

Dafter, Ray. *Project Energy: Running Out of Fuel—Solving the Energy Puzzle.* East Sussex, England: Wayland Publishers, 1978.

DiCerto, Joseph J. *The Electric Wishing Well.* New York: Macmillan, 1976.

Doyle, Sir Arthur Conan. *The Valley of Fear.* New York: Doubleday, 1977.

Dubofsky, Melvyn, and Warren Van Tine. *John L. Lewis: A Biography.* New York: Quadrangle/The New York Times Books, 1977.

Gunston, Bill. *Coal.* London: Franklin Watts, 1981.

Halacy, D. S., Jr. *Earth, Water, Wind and Sun: The Energy Alternatives.* New York: Harper & Row, 1977.

Harter, Walter. *Coal: The Rock That Burns.* New York: Elsevier-Nelson Books, 1979.

Kiefer, Irene. *Energy for America.* New York: Atheneum, 1979.

Kraft, Betsy Harvey. *Coal.* Rev. ed. New York: Franklin Watts, 1982.

Sterland, E. G. *Energy into Power: The Story of Man and Machines.* Garden City, New York: The Natural History Press, 1967.

INDEX

ABOUT THE AUTHORS

Bertha Davis, who has a master's degree in economics from Columbia University, was a teacher of social studies in the New York City school system for thirty years. She has been a member of the faculty at New York University for sixteen years.

Ms. Davis' interest in coal stems from her recent work in preparing for publication a series of articles based on a definitive government study of the effects of strip mining.

Susan Whitfield has authored or co-authored a number of books for Macmillan's Reading Range program. She has a master's degree in education from the University of Pennsylvania and has taught in several Pennsylvania schools.

Davis and Whitfield teamed up earlier for the Watts book *How to Improve Your Reading Comprehension*, published in 1980.